The Rise of Psychomanagement in Australia

Robert Spillane

MICHELLE ANDERSON PUBLISHING

MELBOURNE

Other books by Robert Spillane
published by Michelle Anderson Publishing Pty Ltd

Enlightened Eccentrics (2010)

Questionable Behaviour (2009)

An Eye for an I (2007)

The Management Contradictionary (2006)
(with Benjamin & Rodney Marks)

First published in Australia 2011 by
Michelle Anderson Publishing Pty Ltd
P O Box 6032
Chapel Street North, South Yarra 3141
Melbourne, Australia
Email: mapubl@bigpond.net.au
Website: www.michelleandersonpublishing.com
Tel: 61 3 9826 9028
Fax: 61 3 9826 8552

Cover design: Chameleon Print Design
Typeset by: Midland Typesetters, Australia
Printed by: Toppan Security Printing Pte. Ltd., Singapore

National Library of Australia Cataloguing-in-Publication entry
Author: Spillane, Robert, 1945-
Title: The rise of psychomanagement in Australia / Robert Spillane
ISBN: 9780855724139 (pbk.)
Notes: Includes index.
Subjects.   Psychology, Industrial—Australia.
             Management—Australia
Dewey Number: 158.7

Contents

Acknowledgements

The quotations at the beginning of each chapter are taken from *The Management Contradictionary* by Benjamin Marks, Rodney Marks and Robert Spillane (Michelle Anderson Publishing: Melbourne, 2006). I thank my publisher and co-authors for permission to reproduce our work.

Three chapters draw on previously published material. I am grateful to the editors and publishers of the journals and books in which these pieces first appeared for granting permission for selective republication.

Chapter 3: 'Definitely Drucker', *AFR Boss*, March, 2008.

Chapter 6: R Spillane & J Martin, *Personality and Performance: Foundations for Managerial Psychology*, Sydney: University of NSW Press, 2005, pp252–262.

Chapter 7: 'Medicalising Work Behaviour: The Case of Repetition Strain Injury', *Asia Pacific Journal of Human Resources*, 2008, 46, 1, pp85–99.

Chapter 10: 'Gardner on Leadership', in J Schaler (ed.), *Howard Gardner Under Fire: The Rebel Psychologist Faces his Critics*, Chicago: Open Court, 2006, pp183–202.

For sharing personal information about her late husband, I tender thanks to Doris Drucker. And for reading the manuscript and offering helpful suggestions and support, I record my deepest appreciation to my wife, Joanna.

Preface

Twenty managers spend five days at a management training centre. They are there, at great expense, to acquire spiritual intelligence from their executive coach. The litmus test of their success in sharing this new-age intelligence with each other is fire-walking. At the end of a week of 'energy transference' and 'spiritual awareness' each participant is invited to defy the laws of physics by walking across hot coals. All managers meekly obey and suffer serious burns. Ten are removed to hospital, one disappears and is not seen for two days, and one is found sitting in a toilet with his feet in a bucket of water.

At a management school managers have 'lunatic' written on their foreheads. They are at the mercy of a 'facilitator' who lives in a new age world of natural energy and believes that managers should get in touch with nature. They are told to bow before a lake and thank nature for its largesse. Later that night amazed witnesses try to make sense of grown men howling at the moon. They conclude that the managers are seriously overpaid and possibly mad. They wonder why they are paid at all.

Another training centre specialises in assessing managers' personalities. One brave manager resists and is immediately labelled a 'difficult personality'. A colleague submits to the personality test and is ordered to wear his 'personality' on his shirt for five days. He objects but complies. One week later he initiates legal action against those who subjected him to psychological indignities.

What do these cases have to do with management or the training of managers? They are, I suggest, distractions from the traditional practice of management because the ultimate test of management is performance at work – the achievement of actual results.

Traditionally, if people performed they earned the right to disagree with their managers. Nowadays, individuals who disagree with their managers are likely to be accused of lacking the 'soft-skills' of management. In some cases they are considered to be suffering from a personality disorder.

The popularity of soft-skill management in Australia has re-defined management and created *psychomanagers*: managers who manage by performance *and* personality. I use the term 'personality' broadly to include personality traits (e.g. extraversion), psychological motives (e.g. need-achievement), and various forms of 'intelligence' – cognitive, emotional, moral, spiritual.

Psychologists who promote and measure personality I call *personologists*. Broadly, their aim is twofold: to identify people with 'personality disorders' at one extreme and to discover 'leadership qualities' at the other. This is frequently achieved through training courses conducted by psychologists who use psychometric tests to measure personality. Influenced by new age fantasises, postmodern preciousness, political correctness and feminism, management training has become a standing joke among those who want to be judged on actual results and not on their, often difficult, personalities.

The rise of psychomanagement has spawned a cult of personality which subjects individuals to psychometric tests in the mistaken belief that certain personalities make bad managers and others make good managers, and even leaders. But managers and leaders occupy mutually antagonistic roles and the shift from one to the other is fraught with danger. The manager's authority is based on technical expertise and the leader's is based on personal attraction. Given the behaviour of leaders in the twentieth century, many people have concluded that it is dangerous to follow individuals because of their personality, 'vision' or 'mission'. History tells us, or most of us, that if we follow leaders we are likely to end up in chains behind them.

Using psychology to manage others has great attraction because it offers managers means by which they can control their colleagues. The problem is that psychomanagement requires knowledge and skills that managers don't have. When managers become psychomanagers they have to gain insight into the inner lives of their colleagues, understand various personality theories, tests and therapies. Failing this, they yield their authority to counsellors, coaches or consultants who cannot agree on the most basic issues. And when they attempt to apply psychomanagement they undermine their authority because the relationships of psychologist and client and of manager and subordinate are mutually exclusive.

Psychomanagement combines an emphasis on performance with an obsession with personality and an assumption that the two are linked. They are not. Nevertheless psychomanagers continue to promote the view, discredited by sixty years of research, that personality is important in management. Furthermore, psychologists cannot agree on even the most fundamental principles of personality. Behaviourists and existentialists argue against the existence of personality traits, and psychoanalysts claim they cannot be assessed by psychometric tests. As the heroic teacher in the movie *Dead Poets' Society* said to his students: 'Armies of academics measuring poetry. No, we will not have that in this classroom.' I say: 'Armies of psychologists and psychomanagers measuring personalities. No, we will not have that in management.'

Some managers find the task of making employees' strengths productive too onerous and emphasise employees' weaknesses. Their attempt to eliminate employees' personal deficiencies encourages them to practice counselling in which they are not trained and neglect skills in which they are. Once they embrace therapeutic counselling the roles of manager and counsellor collide. Their point of intersection represents one of the major challenges for Australian managers who are required by occupational health and safety legislation to provide an occupational environment adapted for the physiological and *psychological* needs of employees. Clearly, those who want to manage by performance have had their waters muddied.

The popularity in Australian management of personality, motivation, bonding, emotional and spiritual intelligence raises interesting questions about the changing face of management. How did it come to pass that managers today are expected to 'bond' by howling at the moon, or walk on fire to demonstrate their 'spiritual' ability to defy the laws of physics? Who is promoting this new age spiritualism? Or, as the ancient Romans asked, Cui bono? Who profits?

This book is about Australian managers, their long-standing affair with psychologists, and the rise of the psychomanager. It is written by an Australian academic who for forty years has studied, taught and worked with managers and participated in several of the social movements in which they have been embroiled. It is, therefore, a personal, selective account of a professional life spent studying the problematic relationship between managers and psychologists.

Traditionally, the role of psychology was to provide the opportunity for individuals to master themselves, not to manipulate others. Originally known as moral philosophy, psychology defended the maxim, 'know and master yourself', rather than 'know and control others'. As we shall see, psychologists have been welcomed into management: some work *with* managers to encourage them to master themselves; others work *for* managers to encourage them to master others.

Once Australian managers open their doors to psychologists they enter a world in which Alice would be at home. They are told that they should be managers and leaders, managers and mates, managers and counsellors. They are told that they need coaches, consultants and mentors. When they were confronted with 'epidemics' of Repetition Strain Injury, occupational stress and personality disorders, many concluded that it is a challenging business, managing *à l'Australien*.

Robert Spillane,
Sydney.

For
Maya and Julia

1

A Weird Country

Egalitarianism: The belief that all subordinates should submit equally.

Visitors to our shores initially find everything about Australian life commonplace. Thoughtful visitors, however, shortly find that the subtleties of life in Australia elude them and they become perplexed by its contradictions and inverted emphases. Miles Franklin advised visitors who want to understand the characteristics of Australian life to soak themselves in its atmosphere before arriving at dogmatic conclusions.

English novelist D H Lawrence did not live long enough to benefit from Franklin's advice. He visited Sydney in 1922, stayed for three months, and wrote one of his worst novels – *Kangaroo* – which included wonderful descriptions of the Australian landscape. Lawrence described Australia as 'a weird, big country. It feels so empty and untrodden . . . This is the most democratic place I have *ever* been in. And the more I see of democracy the more I dislike it . . . You *never* knew anything so nothing . . . They are always vaguely and meaninglessly on the go. And it all seems so empty, so *nothing*, it almost makes you sick. They are healthy, and to my thinking almost imbecilic.

That's what life in a new country does to you: it makes you so material, so *outward*, that your real inner life and your inner self dies out, and you clatter round like so many mechanical animals . . . I feel if I lived in Australia for ever I should never open my mouth once to say one word that meant anything. Yet they are very trustful and kind and quite competent in their jobs. There's no need to lock your doors, nobody will come and steal. All the outside life is so *easy*. But there it ends. There's nothing else . . . Nobody is any better than anybody else, and it really *is* democratic. But it all feels so slovenly, slip-shod, rootless and empty, it is like a kind of dream . . . There is this for it, that here one doesn't feel the depression and the tension of Europe. Everything is happy-go-lucky, and one couldn't *fret* about anything if one tried. One just doesn't care. And they are all like that. *Au fond* they don't care a straw about anything: except just their little egos. Nothing *really* matters . . .'[1]

Australia is a land of paradoxes, inversions and sardonic humour. Its paradoxes are exasperating, its inversions frustrating and its humour invalidating: such is life for a people who value liberty and equality, egalitarianism and bureaucracy, achievement and failure, heroes and underdogs. Australians aggressively insist on the dignity and importance of the individual but do their utmost to eliminate 'tall poppies'. Males are said to stick by their mates but will criticise them the moment their backs are turned. Females are said to be tough-minded but immerse themselves in the sentimental banality of women's magazines. Friendly and tolerant, Australians are laconic. Or are they merely apathetic? After all, they repeatedly tell each other: 'No worries'.

These paradoxes are combined with a notable inversion: historically Australians have adopted a cynical attitude to so-called leaders – especially politicians, government bureaucrats and business managers – and have made them the object of sardonic humour. The Australian way is that of the quiet achiever supported by a gospel of relaxation which emphasises getting on with rather than dominating others; it is far more subtle than most observers and commentators care to discover, let alone acknowledge. Valuing their quality of life, Australians work quietly to secure it by defending a status quo that has given them advantages which, they insist, are second to none. Since they see their work as relatively unrelated to local luxuries – the weather, beaches and the vast open spaces – they are not obsessively concerned about economic performance. As for long-term planning, well, in the long-term we're all dead. In Australia the quo truly has status.

The Australian character of the nineteenth century was a mixture of Protestant, Catholic and Enlightenment values. But coursing through the veins of white Australians was European Romanticism. The most popular books in the early days of the colony were romantic: the novels of Sir Walter Scott and the poetry of Byron. As the decades passed romanticism developed an Australian flavour. The bush and bushrangers, the people of the outback and common soldiers at Gallipoli were romanticised and passed into folklore. No doubt this romanticism had strong links to Irish mythology, but it also had important connections with English and German Romanticism. And while Australians would seem unlikely candidates for the label 'romantic' this influence, although it is overlaid with laconic self-mockery, runs deep in the Australian character.

Nowadays it is considered politically incorrect to search for or talk about *an* Australian character since this merely reveals a portrait of dead, white, Anglo-Celtic males. And now that Australia is a multicultural society, it is considered mischievous and morally repugnant to emphasise the virtues (if any) of such a privileged, once-powerful group which dominated and coerced the virtuous citizenry. The fact remains, however, that Australian management in the twenty-first century shows the powerful influence of men and women from Anglo-Celtic backgrounds.

The early rulers of this country had to deal with Anglo/ Celtic men and women who held sceptical, if not cynical, views about power, authority and political leadership (if such it can be called). This scepticism developed, in part, because Australians understood the negative consequences of allowing one's freedom to be surrendered to leaders, governors, politicians or policemen. Australians appreciate the reply of the army officer who was asked to rate a junior officer's 'leadership potential'. 'I believe this officer has leadership potential', the officer wrote, 'I believe his men would follow him anywhere, although it would be out of a sense of curiosity.'

Australians will follow pompous fools to watch them fall into error and then, with a wry smile, allow them to mend their ways. This is the local sport known as puncturing pomposity and pretentiousness, or 'cutting through the crap', and explains Australians' dislike of role-playing. They like to cut through the surface layer of role performance to get to the natural person. And natural men and women are, or should be, 'good blokes'. This approach to social relationships has earned them the vulgar tribute: they don't bullshit. Good blokes combine a down-to-earth unpretentious, self-effacing demeanour with an unapologetic self-confidence. Australian poet Les Murray calls this character *sprawl* – loose-limbed in its mind, it leans on things. Its roots are Irish and it is the image of the Australian character – laconic, democratic and ironic. However, this emphasis on under-stated achievement is often misunderstood or denied, especially if Australians are judged by the sporting people who have adopted American manners.

The stereotypical Anglo-Celtic Australian appears to the outsider as relaxed to the point of apathy. Yet it is a watchful apathy since Australians live according to the 'silence of the law'. This beautiful phrase, coined by English philosopher Thomas Hobbes, describes the strength of liberal democracies – the respect for and internalisation of the law and its universal application. If the law is neither respected nor applied universally the result is tyranny. When the law is noisy the result is totalitarianism, or the sort of communitarianism that is inimical to Australians. So when Australians are referred to as 'wallies' – lazy, self-interested hedonists – one learns to recognise the sound of competing values. It has to be said that in many countries the law is decidedly noisy.

In Australia the silence of the law is accompanied by the noise of celebrities. To be a celebrity, even if only for a day, is an American dream. It can be an Australian nightmare. To survive celebrity status in Australia one must appear to be unaffected by one's success. This means eschewing party politics, any form of formal authority, or support for any paranoid minority. In fact, it is wise to say very little and even wiser to control the temptation to put on a show for an audience unless one is engaged in the activity (usually sport) for which one was originally recognised. Australians respect people who are artless, unsophisticated and unwilling to modify their behaviour for the social occasions that demand it. Their quiet confidence is supported by an almost wicked sense of humour, ironic, self-mocking, incurably sentimental about family and close friends, and tough-mindedly realistic about the external world. And the external world in Australia is tough: the geography presents individuals with unbelievable challenges that usually end in heart-break.

When free migrants arrived in the 1840s many expected to work and master the land. It defeated them as it defeats everyone. But this defeat is the inspiration for much local poetry. Australians are not so callow as to be optimists about life in the bush. Not for them the view that life is, or ought to be, wonderful.

Beyond the cities and the coastal fringe life is indescribably hard and gives rise to pessimism, and even nihilism. But pessimism can be lamented and the lamentations are the very stuff of romantic poetry. And if nihilism is a dominant theme in the works of Henry Lawson and Joseph Furphy, it can be inspirational for those individuals confronted with the abyss because it is for each individual to survive and overcome.

If this sounds like the eccentric German philosopher Friedrich Nietzsche that is because Australia has had its Nietzscheans and some of them have said so – Norman Lindsay for example. Australians have developed their own brand of Nietzscheanism, a tragic vitalism which, unlike Crocodile Dundee, does not win out in the end. The optimistic ending to modern travails points to the commercial motives of Hollywood. Life for battling Australians was tragic, thus Tom Collins' (Joseph Furphy's) final Shakespearean sentences in his masterpiece *Such is Life*:

'Such is life, my fellow mummers – just like a poor player, that bluffs and feints his hour upon the stage, and then cheapens down to mere nonentity. But let me not hear any small witticism to the further effect that its story is a tale told by a vulgarian, full of slang and blankly, signifying – nothing.'2

According to Harry Heseltine, 'nothing' is a word which echoes throughout Australian literature. Presided over by Nietzsche, rather than Henry Lawson, Australian literature is based on a unique combination of glances into the pit and the erection of safety fences to prevent any falling in. If mateship dominates Lawson's and Furphy's writing, it is because behind it was an even more acute awareness of horror and emptiness. Mateship, egalitarian democracy, nationalism, realistic toughness can be seen as defences against the possibility of falling into the abyss. The main concern of the Australian literary imagination is 'to acknowledge the terror at the basis of being, to explore its uses, and to build defences against its dangers. It is that concern which gives Australia's literary heritage its special force and distinction, which guarantees its continuing modernity.'[3]

Joseph Furphy described his brilliant novel about mateship, the bush and local characters as: temper, democratic; bias, offensively Australian. And so it is. *Such is Life* (and much Australian literature) is a study of role-playing and the absurdity of human endeavour. All the novel's characters are playing roles for the role-players they meet. Society is a confidence trick which makes bearable the loneliness of the authentic life. Society is mostly bluff and bullying and those who succeed compromise themselves. Insincere role-players become sick at heart: many of the characters of Australian fiction and poetry are nauseated because their tough-minded realism is unable to contain the nihilism of Australian life.

Norman Lindsay countered the appalling emptiness of Australian life with a philosophy of 'creative effort' which combined the philosophies of Plato and Nietzsche (who do not mix easily). Nietzsche reversed the Western classical tradition by making human intellect a function of the will to power. The intellect is a weapon in the struggle for survival and, accordingly, strives for truth. But the will to power constantly interferes so that the prejudices of classes, nations and religions render truth impotent. Since Nietzsche accepted that truth serves the interests of those with the strongest will, and since will to power is the standard by which human beings develop value systems, he promoted a dual ethic for aristocrats and slaves. The slave morality of the powerless masses found expression in the Christian glorification of compassion. Nietzsche would have none of this and sought to transcend the meek and the mild by affirming life itself which, in its natural form, is red in tooth and claw. But as human beings we have the power to sublimate our barbaric impulses, and create ourselves as a work of art.

In *Creative Effort*, written just after the horrors of the First World War, Lindsay wondered why intelligent thinkers despair of mankind. 'For the years of seeking among the mass of mankind for a direction for man, bring an inevitable conclusion. There is no order, no direction . . . The vulgar expression of Art does no more than refine or stimulate the bare struggle for existence . . . Religion has never served to express effort, but to express emotion . . . No wonder the critic of Life turns from this spectacle sick at heart . . . Seeing the collective stupidity of mankind, its vast, aimless egotism, its irresponsibility, its refusal of all high discipline, and worst of all, how much there is vile and base in it, what can the higher intellect do but shudder and despair? . . . A generation of humanitarian talk and sociological discussion ends in the greatest cataclysm of political hatred and bloodshed the world has ever seen. And after the smoke of this world war, amid the stink of putrefying corpses, and the memory of unmentionable deeds, the voice of the optimist is still the loudest, proclaiming that the Messiah of Humanitarianism has risen at last.'[4]

Lindsay believed that the only way some control might be exercised over man's destructive impulses is by restoring the great classical-romantic values in life and art which had been jettisoned in the early years of the twentieth century. Diagnosing modernist art as a symptom of a disease which was infecting Western civilisation, Lindsay refused to praise and admitted no merit in any modernist. Gauguin and Van Gogh were 'mere savages' who, through their brutal representations, revealed their personal despair. He firmly believed that the nihilistic nature of modernism would ensure its early demise. He was wrong: modernism triumphed and gave way to postmodernism and the decline of *all* aesthetic standards. Junk became art and the few remaining standards by which excellence is judged collapsed.

Lindsay's solution to the sickness of modernism rested with the artists who delve into unconscious life-forces to gain creative inspiration. Creative vision is the ability to discover one's own universality. But we are doomed to failure. All we can do is engage in 'creative effort' and hope that there will be moments of aesthetic consciousness. Agreeing with the Romantics that although we can reject society we cannot ignore nature, Lindsay followed them in the belief that it is up to us to make nature sublime.

In *Creative Effort*, Lindsay introduced Nietzsche to Australians. He firmly believed that the problem of intellectual effort in the 1920s was inseparable from the problem of Nietzsche who found that wherever there was a determined effort to create a high and enduring social state, the hatred and resentment that is the stimulus of the powerless attacked and tried to destroy the higher effort.

After acknowledging his profound debt to Nietzsche, Lindsay criticised him for attempting to create an earthly paradise built on the will of conquerors. He had no time for Nietzsche's idea that if the resentful mob cannot find a direction they must be given one. True, Nietzsche cleared away the rubbish that man had accumulated in building Western society. But having destroyed, Nietzsche fell into the trap of allowing himself to offer yet another version of the great Human State, lorded over by men of indomitable will who, believing that might is right, assume the right to impose themselves upon others in the name of creative leadership. Lindsay would have nothing to do with this dangerous form of utopianism because it presupposed that power over others is given to those worthy of power. It never is, for those truly worthy of power disdain to use it. He was horrified that Nietzsche praised Napoleon: an 'arrogant, destructive little beast'.

In 1932 *Fortune* magazine in New York published Lindsay's opinions of Australians. 'The pose of the average Australian is that of a sardonic cocksureness. He is foolproof: aware of the rottenness of human motives and not to be taken in by them. He derides everything – except himself . . . Nevertheless, this annoying cocksureness of the Australian springs from two of his best virtues: his physical courage and his ability to think for himself in action. For a century he has been forcing a place for himself in a crude and difficult land afflicted by drought and an uncertain rainfall, and the War of 1914 demonstrated his tradition of toughness and endurance. His sporting impulse is one outcome of his passion for taking a risk, whether on a bad horse or by dying of thirst, or casually swimming in the company of sharks . . . Australian churches are almost empty; the Australian spends his Sunday rationally in the open air, and the Australian parsons have the hunted and harassed air of the uncertain wage-earner . . . States of mind do not alter; they merely change their habitat. What was the parson and the convict official is now the bureaucrat. For its size, Australia has the largest bureaucracy with the lowest mentality in the world. The cost of maintaining the public service in Australia is such a joke that one can't laugh at it . . . No one outside of Australia can have any notion of the degradation Australian intelligence has been subjected to by the antics of its official morons.'[5]

Lindsay's philosophy can be called *cynical romanticism*: it is libertarian, pessimistic, elitist, anti-authoritarian and emphasises the individual's detachment from society and politics. By way of contrast, the Melbourne intellectual scene has been one of social, or even utopian, romanticism based on the view that art is central to society and a force for progressive social change. This view is anti-individualistic, egalitarian and socially democratic. John Docker has captured well the difference between the Melbourne and Sydney intellectual traditions: 'The Melbourne intellectual will characteristically think that an Australian, nationalist-derived, social democratic ethos and egalitarian ethic are compatible with what are seen as central values of European civilisation. Melbourne intellectuals feel at the centre of their society, both because they are spokesmen for, or social activists on behalf of, the social democratic spirit of Australia's past, and because they are bringing to Australia European standards of sophistication and relevance.' By way of contrast, Sydney intellectuals 'look to Europe as defining the important and relevant in life and literature. But they do not live in Europe, and if they did, would not feel part of Europe's, particularly England's, actual social texture. Rejecting Australia and in effect rejected by Europe, they are threatened by a complete personal nothingness.'[6] They opt for a third realm where universal romantic European ideals prevail. Since they reject society they cling to the romantic idea of the natural as real in life and the social as contingent. Melbourne romanticism embraces society; Sydney romanticism rejects it.

Lindsay's cynical romanticism was an aesthetic way of wrestling with existential dilemmas. Henry Lawson's was quite different. He recognised the need of man for man in a rough and brutalising country which produces profound feelings of emptiness. Faced with such absurd challenges to personal existence it is tempting to withdraw into comfortable conformity. One can understand the need to invent the idea of mateship to counteract the consequences of widespread nihilism associated with life in the outback. Lawson obliged and so provided nineteenth-century frontier society with a survival technique and twentieth-century urban dwellers with one of their most cherished myths – mateship.

The loyalty of man to man is interwoven with an obsessive assertion of rights. But the passion for equal justice can easily sour into a grudge against gifted people and the desire for mateship can easily express itself by pulling down those who do not mix with the crowd. The ideal of mateship which appeals to ordinary Australians springs, not only from their eagerness to embrace fraternity, but from their determination to pull down high achievers. Thus Lawson's famous lines from his 1893 poem *For'ard*:

'But the curse o' class distinctions from our shoulders shall
    be hurled,
An' the influence of Kindness revolutionise the world;
There'll be higher education for the toilin', starvin' clown,
An' the rich an' educated shall be educated down;
An' we all will meet amidships on this stout old earthly
    craft,
An' there won't be any friction 'twixt the classes fore'-n'-aft.
We'll be brothers, fore'-n'-aft!
Yes, an' sisters, for'-n'-aft!
When the people work together, and there ain't no fore'-
    n'-aft.'[7]

In Lawson's life and work, however, mateship is fragile and conditional. It didn't (and still doesn't) apply to women, children, Aborigines and Asians, although it did apply to dogs and horses. More importantly, Lawson realised that mateship was a protection against living with oneself. Those who deviate from the path of sociability and choose the lonely road of the reclusive individual invariably go mad. Did they need society? But it was the need to escape from the hypocrisy of society that made the journey to individuality necessary. And the result was, in Lawson's words, nothing.

Confronted by the terminal claustrophobia of hypocritical social relationships the inhabitants of this wide brown land had a unique opportunity to 'go bush'. Most didn't. And those who did – explorers, farmers, bushrangers – were generally broken by the bush. Their belief that coming to terms with the bush was an index of one's character reminds one again of Nietzsche: what doesn't kill me makes me stronger. To this day there is a silent and deep respect for those who battled with the bush, and failed. Compassion for the underdog was not solely a reflection of identification with convicts and hostility to their rulers. It had as much to do with the compassion and respect felt for those who struggled bravely but pointlessly with the harsh conditions of the Australian outback. Compassion for the underdog was combined with a romantic view of the people in the bush, even if our romantic writers were mostly disaffected urban intellectuals for whom the outback represented, as it does today, vicarious thrills and a relief from the claustrophobia and conformity of city and suburbs.

The vast open spaces of Australia influence people in different ways: intoxicating for some, frightening for others. While 'Banjo' Patterson glorified life in the outback and wrote heroically optimistic tales, the poetry that plumbed the depths of the Australian character was cynically romantic. For many people the Australian landscape produces profound disquiet in which the individual is truly at one with a harsh, raw environment which so reduces him to insignificance that he feels swallowed up by nature. It is easy to understand why this experience was often portrayed by local writers as a form of madness and why Australians share a deep ambivalence towards the bush. Australians who know the bush acknowledge an intimate connection with each other: their empathy is based on a deep understanding of the precariousness of existence and the need of forbearance in the face of absurdity.

Australians, at least those in the outback, have faced a fundamental choice. One can act as if nothing matters or, while accepting the ultimate futility of life, one can act as if it is not futile. The Australian character has been moulded by this choice. And the result is a curious mixture of the two where today the most common expressions are 'no worries', 'she'll be right' – cryptic and easy-going versions of Lawson's 'it doesn't matter much, nothing does'.

The bush, vast, brutal, mysterious and tragic is a symbol of the outback Australian character as it was until the 1950s. In *The Australian Legend*, Russel Ward described the bushman as 'a practical man, rough and ready in his manners, and quick to decry any appearance of affectation in others. He is a great improviser, ever willing "to have a go" at anything but willing to be content with a task done in a way that is "near enough". Though capable of great exertion in an emergency, he normally feels no impulse to work hard without good cause . . . He swears hard and consistently, gambles heavily and often, and drinks deeply on occasion. Though he is "the world's best confidence man", he is usually taciturn rather than talkative, one who endures stoically rather than one who acts busily. He is a "hard case", sceptical about the value of religion and of intellectual and cultural pursuits generally . . . He is a great "knocker" of eminent people unless, as in the case of his sporting heroes, they are distinguished by physical prowess. He is a fiercely independent person who hates officiousness and authority – especially when these qualities are embodied in military officers and policemen. Yet he is very hospitable and, above all, will stick to his mates through thick and thin, and even if he thinks they may be in the wrong . . .'[8]

A darkly heroic realism developed among pioneers because of the harshness of the bush, which broke nearly all of the hard men and women who tried to master it. Thus there developed among the early Australians a creed of integrity – of being true to life – which reminds one of the cynical romanticism of Nietzsche and Albert Camus. Australian history is filled with tragic stories of lost children, drought, bushfire, floods, loneliness and tragic death in the outback. Australia boasts 11 of the 15 most poisonous snakes in the world (including the top three), the most poisonous spider (and in Sydney too), the deadly box jelly-fish and blue-ringed octopus, scorpions, sting-rays, sharks and crocodiles that have developed a taste for American tourists. And how does the man in the bush react to these nuisances? 'The first march of the young pioneers was over; the sixteen miles of rough uptrack had been traversed in a day; the average load had been over a hundred pounds per man . . . Between the wall of timber and the cliff rim ran an open strip a few yards wide, a breathing space which was chosen for a camp site. Before blankets were rolled out, six tiger snakes had to be killed and two bull-dog ants' nests burned out. Herb had been sitting on the brink of a cliff watching the opalescent spray of the falls leaping out into the twilight. On getting up to go back to the camp site, he found two hissing flattened reptiles blocking his path; there was no stick handy and no retreat. "Bring a stick!" he yelled to the others, "Two snakes here!" "You can have my stick," Norb called out, a bit out of breath, "as soon as I've finished killing these beggars over here." Two carpet snakes and a twelve foot rock python were spared – they proved useful about the camp later by eradicating bush rats. It would have been a bad camp for a sleep-walker; three yards from the foot of their leafy beds was certain death over the three hundred feet cliffs; behind their heads was a tangled mass of thorn, stinging tree and burning vine, which the jungle always uses as a first line of defence; over in the coarse tussocks beyond the camp fire lived a large community of tiger snakes and death adders, which for centuries had been lords of this one, sun-baked ledge on the vast, gloomy plateau. Such trifles do not trouble men who carry a horse's pack all day, and so, undisturbed by the howling of dingoes and the scream of Powerful Owls, the first night passed in heavy sleep.'[9]

Australia is a hard country and the people have had to adopt a starkly realistic view of life, or go under. In the bush, they usually go under anyway. One way to cope with a hard country and a tough life is through humour. Australian humour – realistic and sardonic – is used as a self-protective device to keep one's courage up in the face of inevitable disaster. This black humour involves an ironic acceptance of the fact that in the end, we all lose. Confronted by tanks, a digger said to his mate: 'You go that way and I'll go this way, and we'll surround 'em.' Deeply rooted in disjunctions – English versus Irish, male versus female, bush versus city, optimism versus disappointment – irony dominates Australian humour. Henry Lawson: 'I believe that's how it is, though the man who told me may have been a liar. Another man said he was a liar, but then he might have been a liar himself – a third person said he was one. I heard there was a fight over it, but the man who told me about the fight might not have been telling the truth.'

Casual, shoulder-shrugging resignation leads to the stark conclusion that 'we can't win, no matter what' – the swagman in *Waltzing Matilda* died, the bushrangers Ned Kelly and Ben Hall perished, and many soldiers died pointlessly in the disaster at Gallipoli. Despite this, Australians continue to protest vigorously, and their vehicle for protest is swearing. Ned Kelly's description of the Victorian police is legendary: 'The brutal and cowardly conduct of big, ugly, fat-necked, wombat-headed, big-bellied, magpie-legged, narrow-hipped, splay-footed sons of Irish bailiffs or English landlords.' And our beloved Gough Whitlam: 'I do not mind the Liberals calling me a bastard . . . But I hope you will not publicly call me a bastard as some bastards in the Caucus have.'[10]

Laconic and stoical, Australians combine a calm acceptance of the fates with a grim humour. From Percy Lindsay comes the story of the barmaid who said to professional men, 'Sorry boys, but would you mind keeping it down a bit. Dad's gone and hanged himself in the woolshed.' Percy: 'And sure enough there was the poor bastard hanging from a rafter dead as a doornail. He had his mouth half open in a funny way and looked a bit grim. We had quite a job getting him down.' A friendly drinking session is interrupted by the tragedy of human existence to which those present respond sympathetically but without melodrama. Such is life. The contrast with European angst, English class consciousness and American histrionics is obvious and makes this a very Australian story, even down to the words used in its telling. The barmaid says 'sorry' – a favourite Australian word used to inform unfortunate travellers that buses are out of service. Visitors note with amusement that Australians apologise for things that aren't their fault. 'Would you mind' is obsessively used to avoid the appearance of authoritarian behaviour, while 'a bit' is a popular expression used to qualify, if not further apologise for, the request. Visitors have also noted the irritating tendency of Australians, especially females, to end their sentences with rising intonation as if asking a question. 'We had a lovely holiday?' means 'We had a lovely holiday. Is that all right with you?' In Australia one must never place oneself above others.

Although European romanticism was an important influence on nineteenth-century writers, Irish romanticism was even more influential. Patrick O'Farrell argued that it is not the conflict between individual and the bush, but *culture conflict* (notably between the English and Irish) which explains the development of Australian society. The refusal of the Irish to act out a deferential role discomforted the English elite, eroded their feelings of superiority and announced that the old-world social order could not be reproduced in Australia. This produced a general atmosphere in which rigid hierarchies became increasingly difficult to sustain. It was the Irish and their friends who freed the atmosphere of authoritarianism, pretence and pomposity. The main unifying theme of Australian history is, for O'Farrell, the clash between the English majority (moderate, respectable, conformist), the Irish minority (melancholic, humorous, romantic, contradictory, volatile), and a local Australian minority (masculine, hedonist, non-intellectual). 'In creating new horizons, (the Irish) outreached themselves into a condition of pale emptiness: Australia gradually leached and bleached their substance. In Australia the Irish searched, or deliberately failed to search, for that which was not there – a sense of meaning and purpose. Not for identity. The emigrant Irish knew who they were. It is no accident that the Australian stereotype image of the tall, tanned bushman/digger/lifesaver presented a physical idealisation of non-Irish characteristics: the quick, dark Celt, pale, short and wiry, intense and individualist, defied generic inflation. The constant Australian occupation of image-building went on without Irish participation. Sun-bronzed, masculine, hedonist but a devotee of the cult of mateship, military, wholesome, non-intellectual, and son of sand and surf – Irish qualities are hard to detect in such a mixture. Yet the assumed qualities of national character (as distinct from physique) draw heavily on the Irish: independence, lawlessness; stereotypes that were easy-going, anti-hierarchy and authority, generous, fun-loving, boozy, and game as Ned Kelly. The Irish might not look the epitome of a large and self-confident colonial independence, but they acted it: the frame and flesh of the typical Australian were not Irish but his disposition was. Not so his mind and heart. Those the Irish kept to themselves, rendering the archetypal Australian as a hollow man.'

The English thought that Australia should be a little England of the South Seas, but the Irish minority promoted an Australian nationalism which repudiated the class-consciousness and conservatism of British society. The Irish were enemies of pretentiousness, pomposity and repression, indifferent to worldly progress, and friends of innocent merriment, mischief and passionate tragedy. 'While the non-Irish rich and powerful pursued individual eminence and personal possessions and built commercial and industrial empires that grasped small men by the throat, the poor and virtuous Irish preferred anonymity, equality, and the comfort of their own kind as their vision of a tolerably human life. It was a coherent, morally defensible stand for the underdog, but its danger lay in sanctifying and perpetuating the role of underdog; in courting the construction of a world in which only the underdog ruled, with his strange fatalism, his pessimism, his denial of self, his suspicion of excellence, his sense of grievance.'[11]

Yet it would be a gross oversimplification to suggest that early Australians did not value skill and effectiveness. Nor is it true that they were opposed to authority in all its forms. While Australians oppose authoritarians on principle, they are relatively accepting of authoritative individuals – experts. This is well demonstrated in the case of the Australian fighting soldiers – the diggers – in the First World War.

Known collectively as the A I F – the Australian Imperial Force – it was created from nothing: no history, no elite regiments and no martial tradition. But the diggers created a tradition of their own: unsurpassed courage in fighting, indiscipline on the parade ground, riotous behaviour on rest and recreation leave, constant swearing, heavy drinking, fiercely independent and opportunistic behaviour, masterful use of irony and sardonic humour. Away from the battlefield their discipline was lax to the point of anarchic.

General William Birdwood dined out many times on the following story of his inspection of an Australian camp. Leaning against a gate was a sentry, gun yards away, who showed no interest in the general with a plumed hat. He neither move nor saluted. The general was furious. Briskly he marched up to the sentry.

'Soldier', he said, 'You didn't salute me.'

The sentry agreed.

'Why not?' demanded the red-faced general.

The soldier shrugged at the absurdity of the question.

'Do you know who I am?' asked an increasingly furious British general.

The soldier surveyed him from his shining boots to the feathered plume in his hat.

'No idea,' he answered.

'I'm General Birdwood, your commander-in-chief.'

'Well, in that case,' replied the soldier flatly, 'why don't you shove your feathers up your arse and fly away, like any other bird would.'

In *The Myth of the Digger*, Jane Ross has shown that the diggers recognised the general legitimacy of the army system (as they did bureaucracies generally). But in granting legitimacy to each officer his formal role was of relatively little importance. Legitimacy was granted on a limited and revocable basis. If an officer proved incompetent or did not care for his men, his influence was severely circumscribed. This didn't matter much to the diggers since they had no need of leaders anyway. Ross argued that these restrictions on the granting of legitimacy should not be construed to mean that the diggers were 'anti-authority'. The diggers believed they were entitled to receive reasons to support the orders they were expected to carry out. And it was reasons they demanded and received. For the diggers, the legitimacy of a power relationship depended on the personal qualities of the officer rather than on his formal claims to power as a holder of a commission. While the diggers were not generally hostile to officers, they were irritated by those who claimed more than their due in respect of privileges, or those who gained commissions for the wrong reasons. They reserved the right to rely on their judgement, expected officers to be fair and to issue orders in a particular way. Australian officers had high standards set for them by subordinates who were more critical of those who wielded power than were their colleagues in more deferential armies. But what did the diggers require of their officers?

Australians expected not only military skills from their officers but also courage and common sense. If they didn't measure up, they should be sent back to base. Believing that fighting was a straightforward task which most Australians could undertake with little effort, the diggers resisted training. If almost anyone can fight, there is no need to defer to officers since any fighting man can be an officer. An officer was obeyed if he explained why his orders should be followed. If diggers were satisfied that the orders were necessary and accorded with common sense, they carried them out with vigour and courage. If the orders made no sense to them, the officer had a problem. 'If (the digger) is given an order he wants to know what it's all about. If he's satisfied that it is necessary and that it is common sense he will carry out that order through all the fires of hell. If he lacks faith, then God help the officer.'[12]

While the battlefield abounded with good officers, the base camps had the worst bureaucratic characteristics. Camp officers were obese, lazy, incompetent soldiers who were obsessed with army rituals and regulations. The diggers called them captains of flatulence and treated them with disdain. They were 'broken dolls' and 'staff drones' who lacked courage, initiative, decisiveness, independence, irreverence and common sense. In short, fighting was valued far more highly than administrative skills. Bureaucrats have never had an easy time of it in Australia.

Australians have long understood the inadequacies of action even though they enjoy action. They know how to be heroes without a cause and strive to suffer ordeal sardonically. Dogmatic pronouncements about Australians being anti-authority are, therefore, unwarranted and probably derive from confusing power and authority. Australians recognize the value of authority when they want to know why they should do what is asked of them. Their language might have been mutinous but they dismissed mutineers contemptuously as 'fucking no-hopers', 'fellers who ought to have their heads read', 'bloody fools who had gone completely off their rockers'. They were rebels against hierarchy but obeyed orders if it was *reasonable* to do so.

According to historian W K Hancock, 'Australians are not content merely to attack privilege or to remove the handicaps which birth has imposed upon capacity. Rather, they tend to ignore capacities in their preoccupation with needs. Equality of opportunity implies free scope for natural talent, which must create new inequalities; whereas what Australian democracy desires is equality of enjoyment. Australian democracy has done much to equalise opportunities; but it has also done something to narrow them. It is properly anxious that everybody should run a fair race. It is improperly resentful if anybody runs a fast race. Indeed, it dislikes altogether the idea of a race, for in a race victory is to the strong. Its solicitude is for the weak, and its instinct is to make merit take a place in the queue.'[13] While they are supposed to be matter-of-fact folk who distrust politicians and their rhetoric, Australians have been incurably romantic in their faith in the power of government to fulfil their needs. They have been too prepared to water good wine so that there may be enough for everybody even though most male drinkers prefer beer.

Hancock saw in this volatile mixture of romantic sentiments a challenge for Australians to create their own values and sweep away the old quarrels of the day before yesterday. If the values of the old world were to be rejected, new values would be needed.

It is not surprising, therefore, that several artists of a century ago were attracted to the philosophy of Nietzsche who called for a revaluation of all values. But Australians compromised their romantic idealism and settled for everything that Nietzsche loathed – a 'middling standard'. Nietzsche proved too demanding, too aristocratic and too contemptuous of the average man.

The fierce nationalism promoted by the 'bohemians of the *Bulletin*' in Sydney expressed itself as a vindication of equality and democracy and an assertion of the supreme worth of the common man. Such a philosophy is hardly Nietzschean. Democratic nationalism reinforced with Henry Lawson's gospel of mateship and the romanticising of the bushman by the *Bulletin* school of writers, produced the legendary Australian ambivalence to authority.

Australian attitudes to authority reflect the paradox that the quest for equality has been satisfied to such a large extent by the establishment of bureaucratic institutions. During the colonial era each of the six colonies developed a complex system for dealing with domestic problems, while the British government retained responsibility for defence, external relations and other central government functions. These were transferred to the Commonwealth government at federation, but the states retained many of the most important powers, including taxation, until the Second World War. These peculiar historical circumstances have resulted in the complaint that Australia is one of the most over-governed countries in the world, with many functions duplicated at state, federal and local government levels. Australians believe that government exists to service individual rights so that the state should be a vast public utility devoted to providing happiness for the greatest possible number of citizens. Accordingly, Australians have developed a talent for bureaucracy. In city and the country, where individualism is strong, bureaucratic behaviour is deeply ingrained. Understandably, Australians take a dubious pride in this since it appears to contradict the cherished image of anti-authoritarian, ungovernable individualists. Where is the rugged individualist who scorns authority? On the other hand, with many public servants to take care of their needs, Australians developed as their dominant religion a gospel of relaxation.

In his aptly named book, *Land of the Long Weekend*, Ronald Conway described Australia in the 1970s as the country where weekdays are days of R&R which help the locals recover from the last and prepare for the next weekend. Symptomatic of the late twentieth-century Australian lifestyle was an obsessive dedication to immature consumerism, mortgaged luxury, brick-veneered suburbia and unearned leisure. As a result of the breakdown of family relationships, Australians rejected rather than embraced values and turned to a peer-group lifestyle based on superficial and unconvincing mateship. Australia is one of the highest-ranking Western countries in terms of number of holidays and its administrators have cunningly contrived to have most of them on a Monday. The long weekend has thus become a national symbol in a country where pleasure is linked with novelty and 'getting away from it all'. But what are they getting away from? Surely not a life of hard work since, as every Australian knows, the innumerable underperformers are not confined to blue-collar workers involved in heavy manual labour but include employees at all levels of work organisations. Australians have always been plagued by vagueness, tardiness, incompetence and vacuous unconcern from public servants and members of the (misnamed) service industry. While it is easy and tempting to attribute this widespread apathy and incompetence to the values of Australian workers, it is positively impious to *blame* them for their shortcomings. And the same applies to managers who, one might have thought, play an important role in ensuring that their colleagues perform effectively. Yet for years managers have indirectly encouraged incompetence in their colleagues for fear that direct confrontation will not be worth the effort. The workplace is not a place for work: it is a place to prepare for and recover from the far more stimulating activities of the weekend, especially those concerned with sport.

The national obsession with sport carries with it an affirmation of human courage and endurance where physical achievement is the standard by which individuals are assessed. The obsession with sport, however, seems to contradict Australia's notorious 'levelling tendency': a mistrust of excellence and suspicion of celebrities. As everybody knows, Australians have a decidedly ambivalent, if not negative, attitude to individual eminence and distinction, with the exception of sport. Australians often qualify their comments about leadership with 'except in sport', although that expression is generally qualified with 'so long as they are good blokes': unpretentious, modest, laconic in victory. They should not appear 'uppity', arrogant or self-assertive and they should not indulge in American-style self-glorification.

A major weakness of folk history is that commentators abstract popular values from the local literature and apply them to the general population. Are our profound and lovable values – egalitarianism, mateship, tolerance, friendliness, stoicism, sardonic humour – characteristic of suburban Australians?

In *Intruders in the Bush*, John Carroll argued that there have been three main influences on Australian culture: upper-middle class Victorian values and institutions, working class (especially Irish) egalitarianism, and twentieth-century consumerism. Middle-class Australians settled themselves into British-style suburbs dominated by British-style houses, sent their children to British-style schools where they played cricket and rugby. However, in the late nineteenth century working-class Irish-Australians staged a cultural take-over of English values. At its heart was an egalitarian ethos with an accompanying intolerance of respectability and manners, hostility to formal authority, a talent for improvisation but also for bureaucracy, and a romantic attitude to male comradeship.

Carroll argued that the only thing that is typically Australian about the egalitarian-mateship phenomenon is that it is more widespread than in other Western countries. This ethic has been prominent in Australia because of the peculiar nature and strength of the working-class experience, and the fact that the upper-middle class, including managers as a class, has not been able to enshrine its values. This failure was due not to lack of strength but to lack of confidence. The values and manners of this class have remained the preserve of a small minority. Why did the middle class fail to consolidate its culture? Carroll's thesis is that the formation of Australian society coincided with a general development in the West whereby the middle class came progressively under the influence of an egalitarian *bad conscience*. He argued that democracies suppress excellence and individuality and encourage disdain for hierarchy, which makes it inevitable that central governments increase their power. But above all, the egalitarian spirit of democracies legitimates the envy of difference and of superiority. So the targets of envy establish disarming strategies by disguising whatever is likely to be coveted. This fear of envy is a contributing factor to the bad conscience of the modern middle class. The pressure to maintain disarming strategies may result in a questioning of the very values once so vigorously defended. The Puritan virtues of hard work, frugal living and responsibility for community require committed belief and action. Living in a country lacking in tradition and born of culture conflict, Australians do not believe deeply enough, or in sufficient numbers, in these values. Where the authority of an old culture collapses there is a strong tendency for people to identify with the victims. This is what happened in Australia and accounts for its citizens' empathy with underdogs, the lower classes, the stressed and mentally ill, the deviant and criminal. Carroll noted that this middle-class bad conscience is not new to post-1950 Australia since it was well established in the myth-makers of the 1890s who were, significantly, urban middle class.

Over the past twenty-five years Australian characteristics have been changed by feminism, multiculturalism and postmodernism. The traditional 'true blue' stereotype is acknowledged by a small minority and only fifteen per cent of Australians identify with the man on the land. The majority do not identify with this easy-going, down-to-earth, masculine, anti-intellectual Australian. By contrast, many see themselves as sophisticated, ambitious, hard-working, generous, creative in the arts and sciences, egalitarian, loyal and tolerant. As a consequence of the increasing feminisation of life in Australia males have become more willing to express their emotions. One has only to watch popular television programs to see men crying when confronted with their newly improved backyard. However, Australians have also become passive, soft, impatient with theoretical or complex subjects, materialistic and obese. They demand that their politicians and bureaucrats work for them, but are cynical about their ability to do so.

If Australians rely so heavily on bureaucracy one might expect them to value leadership. However, their cynical attitude to politicians, bureaucrats and managers militates against leadership, at least from them. So Australians live an exasperating paradox: paradoxical because they depend on politicians, bureaucrats and managers but don't trust them; exasperating because they pursue a goal that is doomed to failure. Believing that Australian democracy could, as a local poet said, 'democratise the world', they are exasperated by the failure of government and business to eliminate hierarchies of power, corruption and inefficiencies. Their exasperation is expressed through strident demands for politicians and managers to work more effectively for the people, even though they know they will not. The result is a constant discrediting of politicians, public servants and managers.

There have been no leaders in the country's history who have been able to seduce the Australian people for long, or at all. Australians have managed to combine a conditional egalitarianism with a strong sense of their independence and this has been achieved by a strong belief in universalism in law and an associated sense of fair play and support for the underdog. These assertions need to be qualified somewhat, but for now the point can be made that Australians have been wary of those in positions of power. This is the most positive aspect of the Australian Tall-Poppy Syndrome since it has prevented the emergence of leaders, or at least ensured that their status is temporary.

The Tall-Poppy phenomenon is alive and well in Australia in the twentieth-first century. Ann-Maree Moodie interviewed thirty-seven influential men and women – entrepreneurs, politicians, scientists, artists, architects, writers, business executives, journalists and sportspeople. All but three agreed that the Tall-Poppy Syndrome exists in Australia. Entrepreneur Ian Kiernan: 'The Tall Poppy Syndrome means that the underdog is eventually helped up and those standing too tall have to be pulled down. If an Australian starts to swagger and be elitist, they will definitely be seen as a tall poppy.' Politician Gareth Evans: 'Of course it does, and that's one of the things that's quite debilitating right through a political career. It's the less engaging side of Australian egalitarianism. But the nice thing about Australian egalitarianism is that no-one, but no-one, is impressed by bullshit, by status, by position, by authority, for its own sake . . . But the downside is that anyone who is above the ruck is always pulled down.' Actor and director Robyn Nevin: 'Yes, I think the Tall Poppy Syndrome is a national characteristic . . . I think it has something to do with the fact that Australians aren't great celebrators of success as opposed to the Americans who celebrate individual and collective success as part of their culture and I don't think we have that as part of our national psyche.' Director Baz Luhrmann: 'Per head of population, we are out there in the world in a sense, leading the world. We are very good at leading the world, but we aren't good at leading ourselves.' Author Bryce Courtenay: 'I think a little bit of the Tall Poppy Syndrome is very healthy but as an endemic thing, it's probably very unhealthy because, to use a cliché – and it's one of my own – "when we chop down the Tall Poppies only the weeds remain".'[14]

No one has captured the Australian character better than Les Murray.[15] Combining a reference to the vast open spaces and the local laconic style, Murray sees sprawl as the quality of the farmer who cut down his Rolls-Royce into a truck, and sprawl is what the company lacked when it tried to retrieve the car to repair its image. Sprawl cannot be dressed for, not even in running shoes worn with mink and a nose ring. That's Society or Style. Sprawl is more like the thirteenth banana in a dozen. Sprawl is an image of Australia and would that it were more so. Reprimanded and dismissed it listens with a grin and a boot up on the rail of possibility. It may have to leave the earth. But it scratches the other cheek and thinks it unlikely.

2

Managers and Mates

Laconic: Management style that makes inarticulateness a virtue.

R eaders may well object that this romantic indulgence in literature is anachronistic and irrelevant to the current concerns
of Australians, especially those in the business of management.
After all, these philosophical lamentations were products of the
romantic fantasies of urban intellectuals, not a few of whom
were overly addicted to alcohol. Most Australians know little
of the bush and care not a wink about its existential implications. They are suburbanites who rarely venture more than a
hundred kilometres from the security of home base, except for
tropical holidays. Is it not therefore fanciful and misleading to
burden Australians with tensions and agonies that simply do not
apply to most of them? A suburban existence dominated by the
cretinising effects of the mass media protects individuals from
existential angst to such an extent that Australians can happily
claim that 'we are all individuals' (*Life of Brian*). Of course, it
is possible, and some think likely, that the characteristic behaviour of Australians is a smoke-screen for their inability to
make the dynamic adjustments of which Americans are proud.
The laconic Australian way is, on this view, little more than a

pathetic attempt to ward off the presence of those who have developed consummate social skills which threaten artless folk. To go further, to suggest that Australians disvalue perform-ance might suggest that they have yet to find themselves. Their hollowness, so often commented upon by Asian and European visitors, may be a sad fact. Is their disdain for politicians, bureau-crats and managers a well-rehearsed cynical romanticism? Or is it mere adolescent rebellion?

Distrusting managers, Australians nonetheless demand much of them and grudgingly respect those who demonstrate such personal qualities as tough-minded realism, initiative, physical prowess, courage, sardonic humour. Since there are few opportunities to demonstrate these qualities in their jobs, managers are ridiculed rather than respected. The only people who believe that managers are leaders are managers, and some of them are not sure.

Australian managers have never enjoyed a good reputation, even within their own ranks. Only at two activities are Australians incurably mediocre – government and business. So wrote Hugh Stretton echoing Donald Horne who lamented the fact that it is Australians' misfortune that their affairs are controlled by second-rate men – 'racketeers of the mediocre who have risen to authority in a non-competitive community where they are protected in their adaptations of other people's ideas.'[1] Yet there are, according to Stretton, grounds for hope in our 'profound and lovable virtues': a friendly, not-too-competitive society that is still the world's most egalitarian in manners, if not in fact.[2] The problem for Australians is how to combine our profound and lovable virtues with the pragmatic demands of management.

Australian managers complain bitterly about excessive government control of their business lives. Yet, when companies run into trouble they want the government to solve their problems for them. Sadly, many government bureaucrats have been only too willing to comply, thus supporting capitalism for workers and socialism for well-paid managers. Obscene levels of executive remuneration, even for rank incompetents, have led to increasing cynicism about the quality and worth of managers, even within their own ranks.

Australian managers have been widely portrayed as artless, unsophisticated and transparent. Not for them the ruthless confrontation supported by devious strategies to achieve personal goals. Rather, they are an engaging mix of humanity, consideration and conformity. Whereas Americans are performance-orientated, Australian managers suffer certain doubts. If performance is everything one has to applaud and reward outstanding performers irrespective of their behaviour. And this Australians will not do. If it is true that the English expect to lose at sport with dignity and Americans to win without it, then Australians aim for performance with caveats. Since Australian managers are determined quietly to defend their quality of life, they have been sceptical about imported management ideas and practices, and those that appear to threaten quality of life are allowed quietly to wither on the vine. Direct confrontation with overseas experts and gurus is not the Australian way. Rather, their seminars are well attended, their jargon briefly adopted, lucrative commissions concluded, but the 'new' management models are rarely applied.

One difficulty in trying to understand Australian managers is that, given local values, they are regarded as mediocre *by definition*. Of course it is possible that Australian managers are mediocre *in fact* and deserve their reputation as 'racketeers of the mediocre'. Reading between the lines of government reports and academic articles, it appears that their reputation for mediocrity is based on international comparisons with American managers. Are Australian managers regarded as mediocre because they oppose their profound and lovable virtues to American pragmatism?

Australian managers face a daunting task if they are regarded as mediocre *by definition*. Indeed it is difficult to imagine what it would take for Australian managers to be widely respected and even revered. They are faced, therefore, with an apparently insoluble problem: trying to promote local values, they manage not to manage. Realising that 'getting on with colleagues' is important to their survival they have danced around American-style confrontation in favour of a unique form of humanism which emphasises performance and personality, management and psychology. For many years Australian managers have danced with psychologists. And Australia has produced several eminent dancing partners.

Julie Marshall and Richard Trahair published a valuable record of industrial psychology in Australia before 1950.[3] Of the 1551 articles 332 are devoted to incentive schemes and profit-sharing. By comparison, there were 169 articles on personnel management, industrial psychology (including counselling and mental health) and 88 articles on management training, education, management traits and attitudes.

In 1911–13 articles appeared in *The Argus* and *Australasian Manufacturer* about profit-sharing and schemes which allow employees to become shareholders of companies. This interest culminated in a request in 1914 by the Liberal Workers' Institute to ask the Minister for Home Affairs to provide statistics with a view to introducing such schemes in Australia. Profit-sharing, industrial co-partnership, industrial fatigue and the Taylor system were the dominant subjects during the war. By 1917 the NSW Railway Commissioner was attacked publicly for criticising scientific management. After the war, discussion of interviewing, selecting and vocational training marked a shift towards the personnel function.

Bernard Muscio delivered a series of influential lectures at the University of Sydney on occupational selection, scientific management and work fatigue. In 1920 he published *Lectures in Industrial Administration* in which he argued that industrial psychology should concentrate on the study of 'mental' factors and the selection of workers to achieve the best results from work. In 1924 there was light relief when an American 'characterologist' lectured on his method of employee selection, claiming that he studied character from the proportionate developments of the brain, face and body from which he predicted occupational success.

The most famous Australian in the history of management, (George) Elton Mayo, emphasised the social and emotional factors which influence workplace behaviour. In 1929 he was appointed professor of industrial research at the Harvard School of Business Administration and through the Department of Industrial Research there, participated in the Hawthorne studies at Western Electric's Chicago plant. After an academic career of almost thirty years, he was at his death widely honoured in his native land.

In 1927 the NSW Chamber of Manufactures established the Australian Institute of Industrial Psychology which actively promoted psychological research. H Tasman Lovell published papers on the 'psychology of salesmanship' and at the University of Sydney A H Martin, arguably the father of Australian personnel management, taught courses in industrial psychology to managers. In 1931 the Australian Institute of Industrial Psychology published his *Three Lectures in Industrial Psychology.* After wittily dismissing such pseudo-sciences as astrology, palmistry, physiognomy, phrenology and graphology, he enthusiastically supported the development of vocational tests in industry. In discussing the desirable qualities for successful salesmen, he emphasised dress and deportment, voice, general aptitude and intelligence, personality qualities – extraversion, humour, resilience, diplomacy and self-confidence.

After the Second World War psychologists promoted themselves vigorously. In 1949 the director of the Australian Institute of Industrial Psychology published an article in *Rydges*, 'Psychology – Management's Ally', which focused on selection and vocational guidance. Psychiatry even managed to get into the act when an author praised the highly successful summer school for executives in Geelong, which included a session on 'Psychiatry as Applied to Management'. R J Chambers described the first Australian management diploma course offered by the Industrial Management Department of the Sydney Technical College. To the surprise of many, the course included subjects in general and social psychology.

Also in 1949 Tom Pauling co-authored an influential article for *Public Administration* concerning personnel management in the NSW Public Service which argued for the increasing importance of the personnel manager. A one-time Australian rugby international, Pauling became one of Sydney's best-known personnel managers at Bradmill and Philips where he pioneered, with psychologist Evan Davies, the use of personality tests in industry. I had the good fortune to study industrial psychology with Evan Davies at the University of NSW and worked with Tom Pauling at Philips in the late 1960s. On presenting me with a copy of Herzberg's best-seller, Pauling noted that 'he got it half-right'. Typically, he did not tell me which half was right.

By the 1940s surveys revealed that between 50 and 65 per cent of firms had personnel departments. Personnel developed a more professional character with the development of tertiary training in personnel administration and the establishment of professional associations such as the Institute of Industrial Management (later the Australian Institute of Management) and the Institute of Personnel Management (Australia).

After 1950 a trend in industrial psychology made significant in-roads into Australian management through personnel departments. Crusaders of this trend were the 'human relations' experts who built their case for psychology on the American Hawthorne experiments. They argued for social and against economic motivators. Although the majority of managers had assumed that money was the greatest incentive for employees, they insisted that employees needed other, less tangible rewards. After 1952 some psychologists reversed the human relations position and argued that money was an important incentive. Because of the confusion generated by the debate about motivation and the role of money as an incentive, researchers increased their efforts to understand the relationship between job satisfaction and performance. They concluded that satisfaction with one's job is not necessarily related to performance and job performance may be only peripherally related to personal goals. We don't know what the majority of managers thought about this debate since there are no major studies of Australian managers before the 1960s.

Sociologist Sol Encel reported a survey from 1960 of 100 senior managers which portrayed them as lacking in community leadership, political knowledge, aspirations and achievements.[4] He acknowledged politician and author, Michael Baume, who described business (in 1964) as the most poorly serviced vocation in Australia, made up from the left-overs of the professions. Australia's prosperity, he argued, depends on good luck rather than on any inspired managerial activity. Business directors are 'created out of the remnants after medicine, law, science, engineering, accountancy and now, even the public service, have reaped the taller poppies of teenage intellect.' A worrying feature of Australian managers was their anti-intellectualism and hostility towards tertiary education. Even today one hears echoes of Henry Ford's defensive attitude to education (history is bunk) as managers rationalise their intellectual inferiority complexes with displays of bravado when confronted by articulate and erudite colleagues. Many Australian managers simply lack confidence in their ability to converse intelligently and argue constructively with others and retreat behind a facile pragmatism which sneers at education and promotes dubious forms of training based on the learning of routine skills or jejune models of 'managerial style'.

In the early years of management neither training nor education was required. Unlike members of the traditional professions, managers could scarcely believe their good fortune when they secured well-paid jobs without formal education. Prior to the 1970s when management schools opened their doors, Australian managers were notoriously practical folk who were wary of, if not antagonistic to, intellectual pursuits. They defended practice against theory, experience against intellect, and training against education. This anti-intellectualism, which is characteristic of Australian life *tout court*, is unsurprising given the difficulty in agreeing on a curriculum for management studies. People who have justified their occupational existence (and high salaries) on their ability to survive a succession of bureaucratic jobs are unlikely to agree on a management curriculum. Indeed, one of the more boorish assertions of Australian managers over the years has been their insistence that they got where they are without formal education.

The days of uneducated managers were numbered, however. Late in 1969 the Commonwealth Government commissioned an 'Inquiry into Postgraduate Education for Management'. The report of that inquiry, known as the Cyert Report, was completed in four weeks and tabled in March 1970. The members of the Committee of Inquiry were American academics who recommended the creation of a 'school of excellence' in postgraduate management education at the University of NSW, thus upsetting the Melbourne business establishment. A second (Ralph) Committee of Inquiry into management education was commissioned in 1980 and Melbourne got its 'school of excellence'.

By 1970 five Australian universities were offering MBA-type programs – Adelaide, Macquarie, Melbourne, Monash, New South Wales – and after a slow start they became one of the economic success stories of tertiary education. Some academics, however, expressed grave doubts and considerable disquiet about the existence of management schools in universities. They were concerned that management schools would be unable to maintain academic standards since new courses had to be invented and old ones modified for business consumption. This was forced upon management teachers by the demands of pragmatic, ill-educated managers, increasingly illiterate students and the urgent need to establish lines of professional demarcation. The fact that academics could not agree on the status of management added to the confusion: is it a science, an art, or a practice?

As management is an interdisciplinary subject its academic founders took the liberal position that its study should include 'hard' subjects, like statistics and 'soft' subjects, like psychology. These were supplemented with functional courses in finance, marketing and logistics. Of special importance were 'people' courses which have travelled under many names – organisational behaviour, industrial/organisational/managerial psychology – and, since the 1980s, human resource management. The 'people' courses directed attention to the personalities, motives and values of managers.

In the late 1960s Geert Hofstede studied the values of 116,000 IBM employees in forty countries.[5] He found Australians to be strongly individualistic, masculine, with low levels of anxiety (uncertainty avoidance). Strong individualism means that: the involvement of individuals with their organisations is calculative rather than moralistic; organisations are not expected to look after their employees for life; organisations have only a moderate influence on members' well-being; employees are expected to defend their own interests rather than allow management to represent them; policies and practices allow for individual initiative rather than emphasising loyalty to employers. Strong masculinity means that: organisational interests are a legitimate reason for interfering with people's private lives; fewer females are in the more qualified jobs; females in the more qualified jobs are very assertive; higher job stress; more industrial conflict. Hofstede's results indicated that Australians adopt a self-interested attitude to work, are easy-going in their attitudes to work rules, but give little support to reforms that would require more involvement by employees in decision-making. In short, Australians are generally willing to allow managers to exercise authority in return for economic and job security.

In their 1974 book, *The Australian Manager*, William Byrt and Peter Masters described the 'ideal type' of manager as a person who formulates and implements strategy, makes decisions, organises people and carries out professional, technical or operative work. They insisted that management is not a profession, in the way in which the law and medicine are professions, and argued that Australian managers do not form a political class. They described Australian managers as: dependent on government and overseas sources for ideas; insular; lacking in boldness and initiative; masculine in fact and outlook; conservative and fearful of radicalism in economics and politics; egalitarian both socially and at work; practical and pragmatic; opportunistic; non-intellectual and some are anti-intellectual; interested in leisure, sport and family; critical of politicians and people in positions of formal authority; versatile; materialistic; non-aggressive; manipulative (but not Machiavellian) in managerial style. In the second (1982) edition of their book these descriptions do not appear and no explanation is offered. Clearly, their descriptions of local managers in the first edition were not flattering and did not correspond to the 'ideal' manager found in American management books.

In 1996 I asked more than 1000 managers to rate themselves as a group according to Byrt's and Masters' descriptions. They agreed with them on all counts: the impressionistic ratings of managers by two academics from the University of Melbourne in the early 1970s were almost identical to managers' ratings more than twenty years later.

An American named England compared Australian managers with their counterparts in the US, India, South Korea and Japan.[6] He argued that personal value systems of managers do not change rapidly, even during periods of significant environmental and social change. The Australian managers in his study were humanistic and placed a low value on conflict, profit, growth, competition, risk, success, achievement and leadership. Overall, the Australians revealed a strong degree of *humanistic idealism* and, therefore, a relatively low degree of pragmatism in their decision-making. England asked whether it is possible to combine (Australian) humanism, with its emphasis on tolerance, security and getting on with each other, with (American) values based on high achievement, competence, profit maximisation and organisational efficiency. We might conclude that it is difficult. American managers valued organisational efficiency whereas Australians valued employee welfare and humane bureaucracy. England argued that Australians' attitudes to tolerance, compassion, trust, loyalty, honour, employee and social welfare suggest that they are more embracing of organisational egalitarianism than American managers who vehemently reject the idea.

George Renwick wrote a report for Esso Eastern Inc. on differences between Australians and Americans.[7] He began by pointing to the similarities – the two countries are frontier societies founded by immigrants from the British Isles whose origins are Anglo-Celtic and whose social values are individualistic and democratic. Both peoples are sociable, informal, forthright, practical, inventive, and non-, or even anti-intellectual. Relationships between them should, therefore, be mutually satisfying. But they are not. Confusion and conflict often arise. After trying to work together, Americans often feel that Australians are cynical and undisciplined. Australians, for their part, feel that Americans are superficial and pretentious. Where Americans have friends, Australians have mates. Australians respect and share loyalty to friends and expect deeper commitments than do Americans who place a high value on merely being friendly. Australians believe strongly that 'a man's got to stick to his mate and see him through'; Americans are more conscious of sticking to their job and getting through their work. Americans need to be liked but laconic Australians do not tell them that they are liked. Wanting to be respected, Americans do things which they think will impress others and expect a favourable response. But it is very difficult to impress Australians who are impatient with attempts to gain their favour. In conversation, Australians are cynical, especially when they correct American enthusiasm. Renwick quoted Australian historian Brian Fitzpatrick who claimed that Australians, especially men, believe that words should be used sparingly, or not at all. If they have to speak, they speak slowly, flatly and without expression to indicate that the subject is hardly worth talking about, except to 'get a rise' out of others. And so Australians use hundreds of colourful terms to convey a tone of amiable contempt. Critical of excessive ambition, pomposity and pretentiousness, they resent any attempt to 'pull rank'. Accordingly, Americans see them as crude and critical. When asked about a person's performance or the quality of a product, Australians say, 'she'll be right'. When given orders from an American, their response is passive resistance. Americans believe that Australians consider work to be a nuisance and do as little of it as slowly as they can. Robert Haupt, Washington correspondent for the *Australian Financial Review*, claimed that Australians believe that work is a national joke and people who work hard are likely to attract suspicion. Americans believe that they can do anything if they work hard enough; Australians believe they can do anything but, unless it is an emergency, it isn't worth the effort.

In 1980 I published the results of a study comparing Australian managers' views on industrial relations over a period of twenty-three years.[8] In the mid-1950s, Kenneth Walker investigated managers' and trade unionists' attitudes to the sources of industrial conflict in Australia. Both groups tended to emphasise legal and economic factors. My research showed that although economic issues remained important, the emphasis had shifted to *psychological* factors. Managers were inclined to attribute industrial conflict to personal greed, lack of cooperation and poor team spirit among their employees; union officials blamed the autocratic, selfish and uncooperative behaviour of managers. These findings points to the increasing 'psychologising' of workplace behaviour and the tendency to include personality as explanations of work performance. In this way conflict at work is attributed to particular personalities, or personality disorders, rather than to the relationships in which behaviour is embedded. The tendency to psychologise industrial conflict was strongest among senior managers and reflected a prevailing view that anyone with ability who is willing to work hard can get into senior management and that the difference between the highest and lowest incomes in Australia is neither excessive nor unfair. This view implies that those at the top fought a hard battle to get there and are qualified to tell those below what to do, and the system is fair because everyone has an equal chance to engage in the battle. Historically, Australian managers have used this argument to justify resistance to any dilution of their rights or prerogatives. Implicit in this ideology is approval of and support for the existing pattern of power relationships. In Walker's study the main factors making for industrial conflict were legal, economic and, in principle, changeable. However, as industrial problems are attributed to the personalities of managers, it becomes more difficult to take constructive steps toward their amelioration. This produces two possible reactions. On the one hand, it gives weight to the radical argument that only extensive social change can reduce the level of conflict between managers and others. On the other hand, it encourages those with a more conservative bent to accept the status quo and emphasise the personalities involved in management relationships.

In *The Seven Cultures of Capitalism,* Charles Hampden-Turner and Fons Trompenaars posed five value dilemmas.

1. *Universalism versus Particularism*: When no rule or law covers an exceptional case should the most relevant rule be imposed on that case, or should the case be considered on its merits, regardless of the rule? For example, if a friend breaks a rule should one defend him or the rule?

2. *Analysing versus Integrating*: Are managers more effective when they analyse phenomena into parts (i.e. facts, tasks, numbers), or when they integrate such details into whole patterns, relationships and wider contexts?

3. *Individualism versus Collectivism*: Is it more important to focus on the enhancement of each individual, his or her rights, motivations, rewards, capacities, or should more attention be paid to the advancement of the organisation as a community, which all its members are pledged to serve?

4. *Inner-directed versus Outer-directed*: Which are the more important guides to action, our inner-directed judgements, decisions and commitments, or the signals, demands and trends in the outside world to which we must adjust?

5. *Achieved Status versus Ascribed Status:* Should the status of employees depend on what they have achieved and how they have performed, or on some other characteristic important to the organisation, e.g. age, seniority, sex, education, potential strategic role?

Their results showed that, compared with managers from more than fifty countries, Americans are the most strongly committed to Protestant ethic values – universalism, analysis, individualism, inner-directedness and achievement. Managers from the historically Protestant countries – UK, US, (British) Canada, (Northern) Germany, Holland, New Zealand and Australia – endorsed these values to a much greater degree than did managers from the Catholic countries of Western Europe and East Asia. Like Americans, Australian managers are strongly committed to universalism, analysis, individualism, inner-directedness, but (unlike Americans) suffer certain doubts about the relative importance of achieved status. Americans are more likely than managers from other countries to believe that winning is what counts. But if winning is everything, nothing else matters. In Australia, however, other things matter: how one copes with success matters.

In a later work Hampden-Turner and Trompenaars put the following dilemma to managers: 'The most important thing in life is to think and act in the manner that best suits the way you really are, even if you don't get things done.'[9] This proposition describes a sense of self-worth that is independent of what one's society believes one 'ought' to achieve. Those disagreeing with the proposition give priority to achievement or 'getting things done'. Those agreeing with the proposition give priority to an authentic sense of self. In short, achievement is about what one has done; ascription is concerned with who one is. Americans opted for achieved status by sixty to forty and Australians by fifty-five to forty-five. The British were divided evenly and much of the rest of the world preferred ascription. These results showed that after the US and Canada, Australia has the highest degree of achievement motivation. The authors suggested that this is due, in part, to the fact that as an immigrant nation Australia has great difficulty in ascribing status to people of varied national origins. What matters is not where one came from but what one has done recently and what one can contribute now. Americans are more consistent in their application of achievement motivation, however, since Australians are ever-ready to support the underdog. The more winning is worshipped, the more creditable performers are eclipsed and marginalised. As they say in New York: if you're second you're last. Not so for Australians who are laconic, sympathetic and stoical in defeat.

I had the pleasure of working in Germany with Fons Trompenaars on a course for senior Western European managers. We asked them to nominate the dominant management model (or metaphor) for several countries. There was almost unanimous agreement that the dominant management models were: US – the football team, England – the class system, Germany – the machine, East Asia – the family, and Australia – the barbecue.

It is clear that studies of Australian management values over a period of nearly forty years reveal a surprising consistency in their conclusions. Australian managers endorse a form of home-grown humanism which tries to harmonise work performance with quality of life generally. England's study is important since it is the first to emphasise Australian managers' commitment to an ideology of humanism. Hampden-Turner's and Trompenaars' study is important because it suggests that, while Australian managers are similar to Americans in their support for broadly-based Protestant values, their humanism acts as a brake on their commitment to performance.

The 1990s were not good years for the reputation of Australian managers. The OECD in its 1992 World Competitiveness

Report rated Australian managers as 'ineffectual', ranking them nineteenth out of twenty-two member countries. The Leadership Report undertaken by Monash University found Australian managers to be egalitarian, responsive, forthright, but indecisive and risk averse. Then along came the Karpin Report which was three years in the making and a waste of $6 million of taxpayers' money. Formally known as the Industry Task Force on Leadership and Management Skills, it was established in 1992 and advertised as the most comprehensive study of Australian managers ever undertaken. That it was, but it was also dominated by management consultants, confused definitions, inadequate methodologies and management jargon. And it offered no new ideas.

In February 1995 the report of the Task Force appeared under the politically correct title of *Enterprising Nation: Renewing Australia's Managers to Meet the Challenges of the Asia-Pacific Century* and was predictably critical of Australian managers and management education. The main conclusion was that Australian managers are hard-working, flexible, technically sound, egalitarian, open, genuine, honest and ethical. But they are also poor at team work and empowerment, unable to cope with change and lacking in people skills. The egalitarian nature of Australian managers was considered a weakness because it had an adverse effect on decision-making and resulted in managers' reluctance to confront subordinates with issues of poor performance. The authors concluded that while the best Australian managers are the equal of the best in the world, there are very few of them. Furthermore, Australian managers are perceived internationally as considerably inferior to Japanese, American, British and German managers. Even among their colleagues, Australian managers were judged to be well below acceptable international standards.

Releasing *Enterprising Nation* to the public in April 1995, David Karpin suggested that Australians need to revere their business leaders. He made the familiar pleas for more women in management, best-practice management – i.e. Australians should be more like American managers – and more and better training and education. But the bad news was that there are no 'world-class management schools' in Australia. We need management schools which employ around 110 academics and our little schools are well below that number. Therefore, we are not world-class schools.

Newspaper headlines were predictable – 'Australians: No Brains for Business' (*Australian Financial Review*), 'Report Slams Managers' (*Courier Mail*), 'Schools Not up to World Standard' (*The Australian*). With a few exceptions, Australian journalists delighted in reporting our faults to the world.

Writing in the *Sydney Morning Herald*, Gerard Henderson thought it appropriate that the Karpin Report was launched on the day after Anzac Day – another Aussie failure. He concluded that there was not much enterprise in the Karpin Report and pointed to its bland observations. He acknowledged that the authors asked important questions but their recommendations were pedestrian and bureaucratic. The Report abounds with clichés and tautologies, 'All enterprises are experiencing change as we move towards the twenty-first century.' Well, fancy that. Finally, the authors' indulgence in simplistic theory is embarrassing. For example, we are supposed to believe that we are moving from old to new 'paradigms of management'. Once upon a time managers were consumed by 'vicious circles' but now they are blessed with 'virtuous circles'. 'The essential problem with *Enterprising Nation* is that it bagged Australian managers without defining precisely whom it had in mind . . . As a short, middle-aged Anglo-Celt, I keep my weighty volumes to stand on as required.'[10]

Fred Emery thought that the Karpin Report was a 'deeply disappointing blockbuster'. He criticised the authors for assuming that management is a newly emergent science. Management is not and never will be a science, yet the authors assumed that there is an emerging body of empirically-grounded knowledge that is worthy of the title 'management sciences' which are applicable to anything called management. More importantly, Emery wondered why the authors of the Report did not ask whether changes in the workforce towards self-managing groups eliminate the need for the supervisors who are included in the authors' definition of 'manager'. They assumed that supervisors can be retrained as leaders, mentors and coaches. This is assumed in the face of one fact, which they probably did not know, that in the 1950s the movement to retrain supervisors in human relations was a dismal failure; and in the face of another fact, which they certainly did know, that human resource people do not know how to train the much better-schooled managers to be leaders, mentors and coaches. 'The analysis of the task-force reveals that Australian management is faced with more of the same old challenges; the recommendations add up to more of the same old solutions. Although the Report lists a depressingly long series of complaints about the state and insularity of Australian management education, it can do no more than recommend higher salaries for professors, forming one really big national school of management and capping the lot with a national body to certify management education and "continue the work of the task force". Heaven forbid.'[11]

If it is true that Australian managers are criticised for being insufficiently American, it does not follow that they should replace Australian humanism (which defines truth as correspondence with the facts) with American pragmatism (which defines truth as what works). If truth is what works for different groups, the dominant group's 'truth' will quickly become the received wisdom until a stronger group replaces it with another version of what works.

Australian philosopher David Stove described pragmatism as 'the American philosophical tradition of self-indulgence . . . This is the tradition which William James began when he learnt how to stop worrying about the non-existence of God and start living, and set out to preach what he well named "the gospel of relaxation", the right of "the will to believe", and that truth is what works. O unworthy non-pioneers! It must be a poor satirist who could not make something out of a hundred years of this inglorious national heritage.'[12] Postmodernists, as we shall see, made a *lot* out of this inglorious doctrine.

If Australian managers are determined to continue to promote humanistic values, it would seem that they condemn themselves to charges of mediocrity. Consequently, Australians are never sure whether they are managers or mates. And mates aren't sure how to respond to the increasing number of females in their midst. Is the age of managerial mateship coming to an inglorious end with the progressive feminising of management? Are the hard skills of management adequate to the task of managing in a postmodern world?

The term 'postmodernism' originated in 1960's literary criticism and is code for a farewell to reason. It is a sign of intellectual laziness and a symptom of the crisis of confidence in the Western rational tradition. Postmodernists laud the relativity of truth as a moral axiom and the failure of scientific rationality. In the 1970s postmodernism was dignified by French and American academics and by the 1980s it had swept American and Australian campuses. There were dissenting voices who claimed that postmodernism was an undergraduate affectation which should not be able to fool rational thinkers. But since postmodernists reject the primacy of rational thinking, the charge fell flat.

Postmodernists share a common project: to bury once and for all time the Enlightenment's pursuit of truth, objectivity and reality. Their main target is objectivity which is, for them, the grandest of all Western myths. The world simply does not exist as an independent entity but is an historically contingent product of local linguistic and community practices: the world is effectively *created* by language and society. There is no single world; there are as many worlds as there are languages and postmodernists. Happily asserting that truth is a word which forms part of a discredited language-game which once dominated Western thought, they conclude that our experiences are not of facts but of 'narratives', or fairy-tales, with varying degrees of pragmatic value. Science, they claim, is no more objective than art and scientists engage in self-deceiving propaganda when they talk about value-neutrality in the pursuit of truth. Like pragmatists, they eagerly embrace the view that all languages are equally valid, or invalid. Indeed, standards of validity do not apply – everything is relative, except the proposition that 'everything is relative'.

Postmodernists assume that only absolute certainty allows us to talk of rational belief and since there is no absolute certainty, there are no good reasons to believe anything. They exhibit what David Stove called a 'disappointed perfectionism' which is associated with an irresponsible, frivolous levity. This form of thinking has led to widespread relativism and a general collapse of intellectual standards. How can one rationally respond to someone who believes that no principle of logic is rationally preferable to its denial?

Postmodernists delight in attacking and defaming authority figures, including managers and teachers, and thereby fail to distinguish between rational and irrational authority. Australian psychologists John Martin and John Ray showed that agreement with anti-rational authority statements was positively related to measures of emotional instability and negatively related to socio-economic status and intelligence.[13]

It is well known that authoritarianism is negatively related to intelligence, education and socio-economic class and positively related to ethnic prejudice and political conservatism. What is of prime importance is whether the authority to which one defers has or has not claims to rational support. Rejecting the right (rational) kind and accepting the (irrational) wrong kind of authority appear to be equally indicative of social and personal inadequacy. In this connection the relationships with intelligence are illuminating. Agreement with irrational authority and rejection of rational authority are both negatively related to intelligence, which means that people of low intelligence are likely to accept irrational authority and reject rational authority, i.e. fail to discriminate between what is rational and what is not. In rejecting scientific rationality, postmodernists fail to distinguish between authoritarian and authoritative statements so that *all* authority figures are rejected, or at least regarded with the deepest suspicion. Historically, this attitude was laughed off as merely adolescent.

In *The Undoing of Thought* Alain Finkielkraut noted that this common, anti-rational language is similar to the language of the nineteenth-century Russian populists: 'A pair of boots is worth more than Shakespeare.' You see, unlike Shakespeare, boots don't lie, so the boot-maker should be ennobled and Shakespeare humiliated. With boots (or garbage) as their model postmodernists want to return to their cultural roots in a spirit of minimalist modesty: they aim for *under-development*. This raging nihilism gives rise to an equal admiration for Shakespeare and for the Simpsons. The opera of everyday life is just as worthwhile as Wagner. Celebrities are granted high cultural status and the intellectual life is absorbed into the banality of 'kitchen-sink' existence. Cartoons have overwhelmed conversations, new age psychology has replaced philosophy and a cult of feeling dominates social intercourse.

Postmodernists reject the idea that human beings are agents – free and responsible beings. On the contrary, they are anonymous, neither free nor unfree, and cannot be held responsible for their actions. Relaxed and flexible, postmodernists believe in 'being themselves' and are obsessed with personal meaning but make no truth claims for what they invent along the way. Postmodern persons float. Prepared to believe that anything is possible, they are easy prey for charlatans who have little difficulty in convincing them that the path to self-fulfilment is easy to cruise.

Postmodernists have learned to lisp in the language of congenial relativism. 'Their intellectual temper is (as everyone remarks) the reverse of dogmatic; in fact pleasingly modest. They are quick to acknowledge that their own opinion, on any matter whatever, is only their opinion; and they will candidly tell you, too, the reason why it *is* only their opinion. The reason is, that it is *their* opinion.'[14]

To anyone with even a modicum of rationality, postmodern *bizarreries* prove that something has gone seriously wrong with our thinking. Refusing to accept that there are facts, postmodernists will, like you and me, rush to a hospital with an inflamed appendix and willingly accept the truth of the diagnosis when life is threatened. They will not treat the doctor's factual language as merely expressive or part of a particular language-game and, like you and me, will participate in the very mature activity of asking questions, and perhaps even arguing with the doctor who wants to treat an inflamed appendix by removing their big toe.

By the 1990s postmodernism had infected the field of management. Ian Palmer and Cynthia Hardy note that whereas modern organisations emphasise mechanistic, objective, bureaucratic and analytical forms, postmodern organisations are organic, subjective, democratic and intuitive. Interpersonally, postmodernists prefer relationships to roles, networks to hierarchy, inspiration to orders, community to contracts, empathy to utility, happiness to performance, emotion to cognition, and commitment to compliance.[15] Educationally, postmodernists insist on teaching ignorance since they view education as indoctrination and want it to be empowering. Accordingly, professors and lecturers are replaced with postmodern 'facilitators' who are exceptionally modest in their disinclination to lecture, argue or reason. Theirs is a classroom in which emotions are shared in a spirit of empathy and relativistic modesty.

It would be unwise to claim that all managers who promote soft-skill management are postmodernists, even if it is true that they live in a postmodern world. In my experience, most managers are unfamiliar with the term and have little awareness of what postmodernists believe. Lucky managers! It is the case, however, that young managers, and especially females, are increasingly uncomfortable with the traditional approach to management. And human resource managers are in a position to do something about this. Armed with degrees in psychology and postmodern consciousness, which embraces as many ideas as there are 'interesting' ones, they have changed the agenda of management training. Cognitive intelligence has given way to emotional intelligence, and even spiritual intelligence. Personality has been brought in to play to curb the excesses of the more boorish males. Autonomy has acquired a bad connotation while mutuality has been elevated to primary status. Political correctness is zealously enforced and those unfortunates who question the importance of 'sustainability', 'leadership', 'empowerment, 'stakeholders' or 'ethically sensitive management', are sentenced to the boondocks. Independence has been replaced by relationships and argument has given way to a cult of feeling.

By 2009 there were about one and a quarter million managers out of an Australian workforce of just below eleven million. Males represent 65 per cent of junior managers in Australian organisations, 76 per cent of middle managers, 85 per cent of senior managers and 92 per cent of executive management. Those at the top (generally called 'executives') are very well paid. In 2007 the average CEO remuneration for the top ASX-listed companies was $8 million. In August 2007 the average annual earnings for Australian workers were about $57,400. So the senior executives of the top 50 ASX-listed companies were paid on average nearly 140 times the average wage. And as every Australian knows, many executives receive hefty payouts when they fail.

Distinguished management author Peter Drucker pointed to excessive executive remuneration as a predictor of poor management practice and business failure. In 1974 he declared that an income ratio of 1:12 between blue-collar workers and senior executives was morally and practically justified.[16] He also insisted that performance should be rewarded, not failure. How times have changed!

In the last twenty years the number of managers has increased markedly. The management education industry flourished as the number of MBA graduates increased. The management consulting industry grew dramatically and consultants began to play a significant role in re-structuring businesses and promoting management discourse. By 1990 the Australian management consulting market was estimated to have an overall market value of $6.5 billion. Management was increasingly regarded as the professional success story of the late twentieth century, and many young people sought entry to its corridors of wealth. Since managers need 'physicians of the soul' to help them manage effectively, human resource (HR) managers were given more power than they had enjoyed hitherto.

The Australian Human Resource Institute has over 14,000 members across Australia. The rise to prominence of this once marginal activity began in the 1980s when personnel management, a predominantly male enclave for retired army officers and failed salesmen, was rebadged. HR academics claim that the difference between personnel management and HRM is reflected in the shift from: practice to values; monitoring to nurturing; negotiation to facilitation; personnel procedures to cultural strategies. I will spare the reader the discouraging business of considering whether HRM is 'strategic' in the way in which personnel management allegedly was not, which is news to those of us who worked in personnel departments in the 1970s.

A management school once offered a four-week summer school in which every half-day was titled 'strategic': marketing, accounting, leadership, and so on. I was allocated a session at the end of the third week and, after introducing myself, announced that I taught 'strategic philosophy' and 'strategic psychology'. No one laughed.

The old personnel managers assumed that people have different values and goals and the manager's job is to resolve the inevitable conflicts. HR managers, it is said, assume that people can think and act collectively and their job is to coordinate people for common effort. In the former case, conflict is embraced and the prized managerial skill is *negotiating*. In the latter case, conflict is de-emphasised and the managerial task is *nurturing*.

This new 'feminine' trend becomes even clearer with the debate between the practitioners of 'hard' and 'soft' HRM: the former associated with Taylorism and Peter Drucker and the latter with Elton Mayo and the human relations movement. 'Hard' HRM emphasises managerial prerogatives, the importance of bottom-line results, and the preparedness of managers to take tough decisions. In contrast, 'soft' HRM emphasises the commitment, personality and motivation of employees. Each approach to management has developed its own language: 'hard' means objective, rational, analytic, tough-minded, impersonal, argumentative – *masculine*; 'soft' means subjective, intuitive, synthetic, tender-minded, personal, empathic – *feminine*.

Clearly, there is a tension in Australian management between 'hard' modern managers and 'soft' postmodern psycho-managers. The rise of psychomanagers has meant that hard-skill management (by performance) is frequently supplemented, and in some cases compromised, by soft-skill management (by personality). Consequently, Australian managers are criticised for their insufficient commitment to work performance. It is of some interest, therefore, to discuss in some detail the work of the most influential advocate of management by performance and a trenchant critic of management by personality, Peter Drucker.

3

Drucker and Friends

Management Psychology: The study of ghosts in the machine; popular with managers who use it to manipulate others, but are its first victim.

Arguably, the great debate in twentieth-century management was between Peter Drucker and Abraham Maslow. Drucker believed that good management depends on whether the manager provides guidance in setting business goals and standards, while Maslow favoured the psychological health of the manager. Drucker believed that there is only one style of management: to make strength productive and weakness irrelevant. Maslow believed that a hierarchy of seven needs determines management style, although only five needs are taught to managers since the sixth and seventh are aesthetic and spiritual respectively. This may soon change given the intrusion into management training of spirit-seekers and other lost souls. Drucker believed that the key question in management is: 'What will they contribute?' Maslow thought it was: 'Will they get along with each other?' Drucker emphasised disagreement, argument and contribution; Maslow preferred agreement, harmony and motivation. Drucker believed that the role of psychology in management is to master oneself, not to control others; Maslow argued that psychology is the most important subject for managers to master and apply to others. Drucker focused on the objective demands of the job; Maslow attended to the person's motivational state.

Drucker's popularity with Australian managers has, over five decades, run in inverse proportion to the popularity of management psychologists. While Drucker is rarely taught in detail, I am reliably informed that Australian MBA students are force-fed Maslow in the majority of their courses and Maslow's hierarchy of problems is better known than 'Waltzing Matilda'.

Born in 1909 in Vienna, Drucker studied economics and law before embarking on a career in journalism. From an early age he was determined to leave Austria and removed himself first to Germany where he met Doris, only to lose her, and then to England where he met her again. They married and settled in America in 1937 where Peter taught philosophy and politics at Bennington College in Vermont. From 1950 to 1972 he was Professor of Management at New York's Graduate School of Business and then Professor of Social Science at Claremont College in California. He died at his home in Claremont in November, 2005.

In 1939 he published *The End of Economic Man* and in 1942 *The Future of Industrial Man*. The former book tries to comprehend the appeal of fascism following the destruction of Europe's faith in an autonomous economic system, governed by rational laws and linked to liberty and equality. Fascism and Nazism succeeded because they were 'irrational' and based on a non-economic will to power. The latter book contains Drucker's vision of the central problems and challenges facing the industrial society which would follow the fall of totalitarianism, especially those of liberty and legitimacy. As Drucker saw the second half of the twentieth century, function and status would be determined by one's position in a large organisation in which a new and developing profession – management – would occupy a critical role. But he worried about the legitimacy of management and often upset business audiences by claiming that management is the second largest *illegitimate* profession – and the first is fast becoming legitimate.

By the mid-1940s he was writing about management but knew very little about what managers do. He needed to study managers but was unable to enter their domain. Then, in 1943, his luck changed and an invitation to study management practices at General Motors set him on the career for which he was to become famous. For two years he was able to talk with GM's senior managers, including the legendary Alfred Sloan. He had already formulated his view that managers have three jobs: to make economic resources productive (the entrepreneurial job); to make human beings productive (the administrative job); and to make public resources productive (the political job). He learned from GM's managers how they perform these jobs by setting objectives, integrating tasks and people, measuring performance and developing people by continuous learning. He admired the way GM's managers took responsibility for contribution and rewarded strong performance. He learned that managers are creators not controllers, and that 'leadership' is not about seducing people or appealing to one's personality. Rather, leadership is defined in terms of followers and it is the responsibility of managers to persuade others that they are worthy, on technical grounds, to be followed. It is simply irrational to follow another person because of his personality – that is the path to destruction.

Drucker learned from Sloan that the purpose of organisation is to make strength productive and he never forgot it. He was never persuaded by the pleadings of human resource advocates who told him that what counts is job satisfaction. Indeed, he pointed to the evidence which showed conclusively that job satisfaction and job performance are not related. Many people who are dissatisfied with their jobs are strong performers whose dissatisfaction can be called 'energy'. He did not agree with those who believe that the major problem in management is ineffective communication. The three major dimensions of the task of management are to think through and define the specific purpose of the organisation; to make work productive and the worker achieving; to manage social contacts and responsibilities. Since managers administer the present and create the future they have to be innovators rather than controllers.

Although Drucker was concerned about human satisfactions he did not believe that it is necessary to have friendly relations with colleagues. Rather than emphasise 'management by getting on with others', he advocated *management by objectives and self-control*. The major result of management by objectives and self-control is to produce responsibility and commitment within the organisation. It encourages managers to develop a set of realistic objectives for their work group and for themselves. These objectives should spell out the contribution managers will make to the attainment of organisational goals in all areas of business. Management by objectives develops managerial self-control which, in turn, leads to stronger commitment and more efficient learning. Sadly, when MBO was applied to Australian organisations in the 1970s the moral emphasis on self-control was dropped and it became management by objectives and the manager's control.

Drucker learned from his study of GM that there are three forces of mismanagement: the specialised work of managers which encourages them to pursue specialised training rather than the general, humanistic education which is essential for community leadership; the existence of hierarchy in which people define themselves as supervisors rather than managers; and the confusion about the organisation's mission. Management by objectives can overcome these deficiencies by relating the task of each manager to the overarching goals of the business. Only by this technique can management become a cohesive group activity rather than a loose-knit collection of individuals pursuing their own agendas. Business debacles, such as Enron, are management and moral failures: they result from the lack of a cohesive management group and the lack of an overarching moral framework to regulate that group.

The business enterprise needs a principle of management that gives full scope to individual strength, a common direction to effort, and replaces external control with more effective internal control. However, Drucker believed that many managers have failed to take the initiative and in emphasising external control they have failed to take advantage of the strengths of people. Employees in most companies are basically under-employed: their responsibility does not match their capacity. Employees must be held responsible for setting the goals for their own work and for managing themselves. This is not being permissive and it is not participative management, which is often only a futile attempt to disguise the reality of employee impotence through psychological manipulation. Imposing responsibility on employees – for continuous improvement in the performance of their own work – strengthens management because it creates a better understanding of management decisions and practices throughout the workforce.

Drucker also learned that, when taking important decisions, argument must be encouraged. A favourite story is of Alfred Sloan putting an expensive and innovative proposal to his board only to have every board member politely agree with him. Sloan deferred the decision for one month to give his colleagues time to prepare arguments against it. After a robust debate the proposal was rejected. Sloan and Drucker approved.[1] Managers are not paid to share their feelings with each other: they are paid to give reasons to support their views. They are paid to *argue* and this crucial ability must be encouraged at all levels of the organisation.

In 1946 Drucker published an account of his study of GM. *Concept of the Corporation* became an immediate success and started the vogue for 'decentralisation'. Sloan immediately banned the book and forbad his executives to discuss it in his presence. Ford, on the other hand, embraced its ideas. When the young Henry Ford replaced his senile grandfather, he embraced *Concept of the Corporation* as his official text and gave Drucker the confidence to develop his ideas on management further. This he did in 1954 in his feisty book, *The Practice of Management*, which is widely regarded as his best management book, and the first and last word on management.

Of all his work on management Drucker considered his ideas about the self-governing plant community to be both the most important and the most original. Managers, however, have opposed these ideas as an 'encroachment' on their authority and trade unions have remained sceptical. Again, it was during his time at GM in the 1940s that he saw at first hand the possibilities for what became known as the Scandinavian semi-autonomous work group movement of the 1970s.

GM had successfully bid for a government contract which demanded highly skilled mechanics. Since there was no labour available in Detroit two thousand black prostitutes were hired. On their arrival they were shown a hastily made training film and left to organise the work in their own way. Within a few weeks these unskilled, unsupervised illiterates were producing better work than skilled machinists had done before. When the war ended and the women were discharged many tried to commit suicide, and quite a few succeeded. Drucker argued that what was achieved in those factories in World War II went beyond the widely publicised Swedish experiments with semi-autonomous work groups in Volvo, Saab and elsewhere. And in these factories neither management nor trade unions suffered any impairment of authority or prosperity. Yet he was forced to concede that he was naive to expect that self-governing plant communities would be supported by managers and trade unionists. The movement towards responsible autonomy at work failed: vested interests are simply too powerful.

Drucker also participated in a workers' survey which was framed as a contest – My Job and Why I Like It – with many small prizes and judges to award them. The contest fully supported his assumptions which were later popularised by Frederick Herzberg as the 'motivation-hygiene theory'. The results showed that the extrinsic rewards for work – pay or promotion, say – are what Herzberg called 'hygiene factors' because dissatisfaction with them is a powerful de-motivator, but satisfaction with them is not especially important and an incentive to few. Achievement, contribution and responsibility are the powerful motivators. The survey also showed that employees want the chance to achieve at work and they particularly resent being prevented by meddlesome managers from doing the work for which they are paid.

Around 200,000 GM employees participated in the contest but its success killed it. It was impossible to read, let alone collate, all the data and the union became so alarmed at the success of the contest that they made dropping further work on it a condition of accepting a wage settlement without a strike in 1948. And so the richest research material on employee attitudes and values ever collected was lost.

After the success of *The Practice of Management* in the mid-1950s Drucker became the most famous management consultant in America. Yet he was never tempted to become Peter Drucker Inc. He remained a 'one-man gunslinger' and surprised clients by delivering his 'reports' orally. As he was leaving a client asked whether he would submit a written report. Drucker was clearly amused and offered to throw in sex and violence to make this unnecessary task more interesting. He was often accused of making 'facts' up and basing his recommendations on anecdotes and novels. His widow, Doris, told me recently that he wanted to be a gentleman in the style of a Jane Austen character and one can see him in his later years as a playful Mr. Bennett. A master of the witty aphorism and a masterful storyteller, he nonetheless maintained a healthy scepticism about the management fads and fashions that followed him. He never accepted the emphasis that managers place on 'potential' since we have all been on promises. He emphasised performance over potential and was especially opposed to assessing potential by psychometric tests. He was equally sceptical about managers' obsession with leadership: 'leadership' often means the ability to bewitch the led.

According to Drucker business has only two functions: marketing and innovation. Sadly, managers are obsessed with organisational structures ('organitis') and after several decades in the consulting business he concluded that far too much reorganisation goes on. He compared organitis to a spastic colon and organisational restructures to surgery: one doesn't just cut. He may have been one of management's greatest supporters but he was always ready to offer constructive criticism. It may surprise many people to hear him say: so much of what we call management consists in making it difficult for people to work; job enrichment has been around for more than sixty years and while it has been successful every time it has been tried, managers are not interested; management by objectives works if managers know the objectives but ninety percent of the time they don't.

He retained a healthy scepticism about professions. He advised his clients not to put the fate of their business in the delusions of economists. He reminded them that there are no good executive compensation plans: there are only bad and worse ones. Many of his clients thought he was frivolous when he told them that if they want to hire fifty people under the age of 25, they should hire double that number at random and six months later sell the worst fifty to their competitors. If they want to hire people over the age of 25, the only criterion for selection is successful performance in the last job(s).

Drucker was, however, a defender of the most maligned man in management classrooms. If managers and their teachers do not like a writer it is usually because he is a critic of their profession. Most of the management icons are sympathetic to the plight of managers and believe that they generally act rationally and wisely. Any writer who believes that managers are generally irrational, status-seeking, power-hungry individuals who make it difficult for people to do their work is a strong candidate for infamy. There was such a man – Frederick Taylor – and to the surprise of many of his students and clients, Drucker defended him.

In the nineteenth century managers were largely concerned with production techniques and the problems of financial control. The human aspects of work were either ignored or given little credence. Among the developments that forced managers to think in wider terms was bureaucratisation. As the size of business organisations grew managers began to think of problems of employee morale and communication, lines of authority and the control of large numbers of people. Managers had also to cope with the loss of individual power: no longer did one individual control the organisation. Individual desires were tempered by committees and conferences which led to a desire to understand the psychological aspects of workplace behaviour.

Frederick Winslow Taylor, the founding father of the 'science of work', loathed inefficiency and management incompetence. In 1912 he described US Steel's managers as shameful and deplorable. He believed managers were generally incompetent because they lacked information about their employees' abilities and the time required to perform their work. He saw that managers arbitrarily designed jobs which encouraged employees to collude to achieve reduced time rates. Managers were selfish, ignorant and irrational. Workers, on the other hand, generally pursued rational strategies of self-interest. Given a hostile and difficult work environment, Taylor found it easy to accept go-slow tactics and self-interested behaviour. He believed that many of these problems could be solved by the application of scientific principles to workplace behaviour since science enables engineers to capitalise on employees' rationality by establishing objective standards for work behaviour. The first step was to study work time, individual work movements, fatigue factors, job routines, work sequences and the timing of rest pauses. Work analysis was, therefore, to form part of an overall scheme which would replace arbitrary work design with scientific principles. Taylor died during the early phase of this ambitious program.

Taylor's writings on 'scientific management', including his five-day Testimony in 1912 before a Committee of the House of Representatives, are reprinted in *Scientific Management*. His Testimony presented his mature views and demonstrated his obsession with substituting industrial harmony for industrial warfare. This would require increasing wages, decreasing physical stress, developing the human being, and replacing 'bosses' with 'servants of workmen' whose duty is to help workers perform more effectively.

Programmes for increasing the productivity of labour through techniques of time, motion and cost analysis were reinforced by the assumption that the major motivating force for employees (and managers) is money, and this resulted in an emphasis on wages, incentives and a 'fair day's work for a fair day's pay'. Taylor and his disciples viewed payment by results programmes and incentive bonuses as adequate compensation for whatever constraints on human satisfaction such techniques might generate. The bad news for managers was that they were supposed to allow some workers to earn more money than they were receiving since Taylor insisted that there should be no limit to the earnings of high-output workers. This they were not prepared to do. To be fair to Taylor, it should be remembered that he warned managers that financial rewards were only a partial answer to the problem of employee motivation.

It is standard practice for management writers to criticise Taylor. Indeed, he has few defenders. One notable exception was Drucker who argued that there are few cases in intellectual history where what a person actually said and did, and what he is generally believed to have said and done, are so totally at variance.[2] Taylor was not solely interested in profits and costs and he did not invent and subordinate workers to the production line. And he definitely did not want to put more power into the hands of managers. Rather, his central concern was to achieve industrial harmony through higher productivity. He believed that workers should receive the full benefit of higher productivity whether in the form of higher wages or shorter hours of work, and financial incentives were necessary but not sufficient to motivate workers. He wanted to replace the 'boss' with what is known as matrix organisation. Contrary to popular belief, hierarchical organisation structures run counter to Taylor's principles. He never hesitated to criticise managers who wanted to centralise power in their own hands. Why, then, has Taylor been so totally misrepresented?

Drucker dismissed the facile suggestion that Taylor was a 'captive of nineteenth-century psychology' which was influenced by social Darwinism and a general belief that social reforms should be grounded on maximising industrial output through hard work and the application of scientific principles. On the contrary, Taylor was ahead of his time in anticipating the psychological theories of McGregor and Herzberg. Yet he was rejected and ridiculed by university professors and by the ideologues of the Left and Right. He died before he could turn his attention to senior managers and we can only ponder what he would have made of today's managers. Have they learned from Taylor about the complicated relationship between money, motivation and manipulation?

A case in point was Henry Ford who, in 1914, doubled the wages of his employees in an attempt to 'hold the workers'. Ford found, however, that staff turnover had risen again by 1918. The cost of living had risen by 78 per cent above the 1914 level although Ford had not increased wages. Instead he lectured his employees about loyalty and gratitude. Finally, in 1920, the Ford profit-sharing plan was abandoned and the search was on for a different approach to employee motivation. It was the Hawthorne studies that were to provide the new emphasis. And it was the Hawthorne researchers who radically modified management ideology. Henceforth, Taylor would be portrayed as the 'bad boy' of industrial work and a new band of social scientists insinuated themselves into management. They became known as the 'human relations school' and their influence was, and continues to be, staggering.

The father of the human relations movement was Elton Mayo who popularised the Hawthorne studies. These infamous studies were conducted between the mid-1920s and the late-1930s at the Hawthorne plant of the Western Electric Company in Chicago. The researchers attached limited importance to formal organisation and technology and emphasised the informal relationships between people at work, especially conditions for sociability and belongingness. The emphasis was linked to Mayo's view that the basic problem of industrial society is best defined as the severance of the social links that characterise pre-industrial society. As increased anomie at work was seen as *the* problem, researchers attempted to generate a social environment around the individual.

The key findings which emerged from the Hawthorne studies provided major themes for human relations writers in their search for supportive work environments: the importance of social norms; the significance of non-economic rewards; the influence of informal groups; the role of leadership in enforcing group norms; and the importance of participation in decision making. The Hawthorne researchers concluded that there was no evidence that workers are primarily motivated by economic interests, and the efficacy of a wage incentive was so dependent on its relation to other factors that it was impossible to consider it as having an independent effect on workers.

Sydney psychologist Alex Carey concluded that there is no evidence for such conclusions. He also criticised the Hawthorne researchers for their refusal to consider the power relationships that defined the work environment. To recognise the power relationships in the factory is to acknowledge the existence of conflicting interests, which the researchers failed to admit or consider. The researchers also ignored the existence of trade unions throughout the study because they were unnecessary. This capacity to ignore management-union relationships was amazing when it is remembered that from 1933–1936, according to a 1937 US Senate Committee, Western Electric's managers paid $26,000 to spies commissioned to report on and subvert union involvement among employees. It is clear that an anti-union, pro-management bias permeated all those who were involved in the nine-year research programme so that interpretations of their findings should be treated with care, to say the least in the most charitable fashion. The other important consequence of the neglect of power relationships, aided by the severity of the economic depression, concerned the status of money as a motivating factor. A demand by workers for higher wages would constitute a conflict of interest and so power relationships would have to be considered. As this was to be avoided within the research, emphasis was displaced from economic incentives to social relationships.

Why such claims as those of the Hawthorne researchers should have gained widespread acceptance is a question in need of an answer. Carey concluded that there are no grounds in the objective content of the records of the Hawthorne studies for their authors' conclusions. The data from these studies, far from supporting the human relations approach, are surprisingly consistent with a rather old-world view about the value of monetary incentives, driving management and discipline. 'It is only by massive and relentless reinterpretation that the evidence is made to yield contrary conclusions. To make these points is not to claim that the Hawthorne studies can provide serious support for any such old-world view. The limitations of the Hawthorne studies clearly render them incapable of yielding serious support for any sort of generalisation whatever. If the assessment of the Hawthorne studies offered here is cogent, it raises some questions of importance for university teachers, especially for teachers concerned with courses on industrial organisation and management. How is it that nearly all authors of textbooks who have drawn material from the Hawthorne studies have failed to recognise the vast discrepancy between evidence and conclusions in those studies, (and) have frequently misdescribed the actual observations and occurrences in a way that brings the evidence into line with the conclusions . . . ?[3]

This is vintage Carey, as those of us who had the good fortune to be taught by him can testify. He told me that he had great difficulty in publishing his paper on the Hawthorne studies and had to settle for the *American Sociological Review*, which guaranteed that few Australians would read it.

Alex Carey was a major figure on the Sydney industrial psychology scene, especially in the 1960s and 70s. His radical critiques of mainstream industrial psychology unsettled and upset managers and ensured that his status would be that of an eccentric outsider. He was a liberal humanist and an inspiring educator but had little time for students who wanted merely to be trained. He arrived for our first class with hair dripping from saltwater and told his class of (1960s) blue-suited managers that we could leave immediately if we thought he was going to tell us how to make money by manipulating others. He was one of the best teachers I ever had and after I graduated from the University of NSW we became casual friends. In 1988 we were asked to share a lecture platform at the then Kuringai College of Advanced Education. My reluctance to attend vanished when I heard that Alex would be attending. He was known for his casual attitude to appointments and so we were not surprised when he had not arrived in time for the session. We were to learn later that at the very time he was to speak to the audience, he hanged himself.

In the field of management Alex Carey is especially remembered for his critiques of the Hawthorne studies and the classic study of autocratic and democratic supervisory styles conducted by Kurt Lewin, a refugee from Nazi Germany who went to America determined to promote the ideals of democracy in all its forms. He drew a sharp distinction between democratic and autocratic styles of supervision and sought evidence for the superiority of the former.[4] He argued that autocrats: determine policies themselves and dictate techniques and activities intermittently so that future steps are always uncertain; are personal in their praise and criticism of the work of group members; remain aloof from active group participation except when demonstrating tasks. Democrats: encourage group discussion and decision; sketch general steps to achieve group goals; suggest possible courses of actions; allow people to work with whomever they choose; are objective in their praise and criticism; try to be a regular member of the group in spirit without taking over the work of others.

It is widely believed that Lewin's studies found that the democrats developed higher levels of 'morale' in their groups than did the autocrats. Further, it is generally accepted that the democratically managed groups achieved the higher level of output. There have been few major criticisms of this study and again it was Alex Carey who showed that the results point to the conclusion that the autocratic groups produced *less* aggression and *higher* levels of output than did the democratic groups. Carey concluded: 'It is a considerable tribute to the experimenters' attachment to the word "democracy" (both in its political connotations and in the sense in which a human relations supervisory style in industry is called democratic) that they are able to interpret this evidence in a way favourable to democracy and conclude that it was more efficient and produced less frustration, less aggression or both. But it is even more remarkable that for thirty years subsequently unending versions of this trivial and worthless study have been spread over literally thousands of pages of journals, books, textbooks, and citations – ranging from education and industrial psychology to international relations. After a time it was widely reported, in textbooks and articles, that output was highest in the democratically-led groups.'[5]

The Lewinian researchers made it a condition of autocracy that the supervisor only revealed to group members the steps to the group goal one at a time, whereas in the democratic condition the path to the group goal was a matter of discussion and decision. But the lack of a group goal is not fundamental to autocracy. Totalitarian governments often make the goals of their countries quite explicit while in some democracies social goals are frequently unclear.

Australian psychologists Adrienne Hall and Pat Bazeley repeated the Lewinian studies paying particular attention to goal clarity. Hall, for example, examined the relationship between group morale, effectiveness and supervisory style when goal perspective was equally clear in both autocratic and democratic conditions and found that there was no difference in morale between the groups. Autocratic groups, however, produced higher levels of output. These results, in conjunction with those of Bazely, offer convincing evidence that clarity of goal perspective rather than supervisory style was the major variable in Lewin's study.[6]

Drucker was particularly sceptical of the 'human relations' and democratic supervision movements. He claimed that the human relations movement grew out of attempts to subvert the growth of trade unions by pretending that managers cared about the psychological needs of their employees. In a 1950 article, he argued that 'The human relations policies which American management had been buying wholesale in the past ten years have been a conspicuous waste and failure, in my opinion . . . Most of us in management . . . have instituted them as a means of busting the unions. That has been the main theme of these programmes. They are based on the belief that if you have good employee relations the union will wither on the vine.'[7] The intrusion into management of this form of psychology was dangerous and had the potential to undermine managerial authority. While he acknowledged that people had different personalities and needs, he was not convinced that personality or motivational factors should determine how managers relate to their subordinates. And he vigorously opposed the use of psychological interviews and psychometric tests. This did not mean that he ignored good manners. Working with people is difficult, but not impossible. Tax accountants aren't going to change, but at least they can learn to say 'good morning'. He believed that if managers spend more than ten percent of their time on 'human relations', they have time on their hands. And to depend on human resource managers to do management development is a misunderstanding: it is the job of managers to develop their staff.

It was during the 1950s that some psychologists worried about the management bias of their colleagues and reversed the traditional position. Instead of trying to show managers how to induce workers to work harder and more harmoniously for less money, they insisted that money was the single greatest incentive. The cycle had been completed. This time managers, following Ford's lead, were not quite as receptive to the 'money' argument. Rather, new approaches were eagerly sought. Personality and intelligence testing, variations on the Hawthorne studies, sensitivity groups, communication techniques, worker participation schemes and a host of managerial fads invaded workplaces. Little attention was given to such subjects as merit-rating schemes, incentive payment systems or wage review programs. The human relations movement may have passed into the human resources movement but its legacy remained. Never again would managers emphasise the motivating power of money. They had flirted with psychologists and they were now ready seriously to embrace them. Psychologists returned the favour and set their sights on the old guard, notably Taylor and Drucker.

Drucker was criticised by psychologists, including Maslow and McGregor, for failing to appreciate and account for individual differences, especially personal needs. Drucker addressed this issue in his 1977 best-seller, *Management*, by criticising industrial psychologists for their simplistic accounts of workplace behaviour and their habit of pretending that descriptions of everyday behaviour are universal theories of human nature.

McGregor had argued that when managers take decisions they make assumptions about human behaviour which reflect their commitment to one of two schools of thought – scientific management and human relations. Theory X represents the traditional, scientific management approach which assumes that most people have an inherent dislike of work which they will strive to avoid at all cost. They work to satisfy physiological and safety needs, primarily through financial gain and since they are motivated by the threat of punishment, they must be coerced and controlled in order to ensure effective performance. Theory X takes no heed of individuals' personal desires to achieve self-respect or self-actualisation. Theory Y, which is more akin to the human relations school, assumes that people will exercise self-control in working towards objectives to which they are committed. It assumes that most people strive for personal growth and responsibility and are motivated by esteem and self-actualisation needs which, if met, satisfy both personal and organisational ends. In short, Theory X assumes immaturity and Theory Y assumes that people want to be adults. Although McGregor presented these theories as viable alternatives, it is clear that he committed himself to Theory Y.

Drucker acknowledged that McGregor's 1960 book, *The Human Side of Enterprise* was (for the next two decades) the most widely read and most often quoted book in the field of industrial psychology. McGregor's research revealed that organisations which were low in efficiency tended to be controlled by people who were 'job centred'. They concentrated on keeping their subordinates busily engaged in a specified work cycle, at a satisfactory rate, determined by time standards. By contrast, the best performances were found in organisations where supervisors focused on the human aspects of their subordinates' problems and saw their role as helping them to do their work effectively. The supervisors who employed a Theory Y approach exercised a general rather than a detailed control over the job and were more concerned with targets than methods.

They had high performance goals but allowed maximum participation in decision making and were 'employee' rather than 'job' centred.

Drucker used one psychologist to criticise another. He pointed out that Maslow had spent a year working with a small company in California which tried to practice Theory Y and discovered that the demand for responsibility and achievement sometimes exceeded what any but the strong and healthy person could take. He criticised Theory Y for 'inhumanity' to weak and vulnerable people who cannot take on the self-discipline which Theory Y demands. He rejected McGregor's assumption that most people want to be adults: many want to remain immature. Maslow concluded, and Drucker agreed, that while Theory Y is superior to Theory X, managers have to replace the security of the latter with a different structure of security which goes well beyond it. Theory Y cannot simply be substituted for Theory X: it has to go far beyond it. He concluded that the debate over the validity of Theory X versus Theory Y is a sham battle. The question managers need to ask is not, 'which theory of human nature is the correct one?' Rather, the right question is: 'what is the reality of my situation and how can I discharge my task of managing subordinates?'

Drucker set himself against those psychologists who treat people as bundles of relatively fixed dispositions – personality traits and psychological needs. He was a sort of existentialist who believed that humans are strategic beings who strive for autonomy but must also be part of society. He was fond of the father of Christian existentialism, Danish philosopher Soren Kierkegaard, who believed that human existence is possible only in perpetual tension between the individual's autonomous existence and as a citizen in society.[8] Like Kierkegaard, Drucker reasserted the existence of individuals against the social conditions which threaten to encapsulate them and he rejected the notion of personality as a psychological trap which submerges individuals in biological and social structures. Humans are never devoid of *choice* and are therefore responsible for the consequences of their choices insofar as they are aware of them.

Management is neither science nor art. It is a practice and it can be taught. But training is not enough. Managers need to be educated for positions of community responsibility and for more than two thousand years it has fallen to the liberal arts to achieve this noble goal. So when Drucker retired from New York University he chose to continue to teach at a liberal arts college in California. To retire was, for him, a death sentence and since he loved to teach he continued into his nineties to face classes of respectful students.

He remained to the end of his life a teacher of rare wit, intelligence and insight into the discipline of management, a discipline which he largely created. He believed that his greatest strength as a consultant was to ask a few basic questions. If a client leaves a room feeling he has learned a lot, Drucker concluded that the client is either stupid or he had done a bad job.

4

Motivation and Manipulation

Manipulation: Comes between managing director and manual worker.

Acentral concept in the debate between Drucker and Maslow is 'motivation'. Drucker quipped: 'We know nothing about motivation; all we know can do is write books about it'. Maslow, who was not known for his sense of humour, was infuriated. He accused Drucker of ignoring psychological differences between people at work, especially issues of personality and motivation.

Motive is a term which has had a variety of meanings in the course of history. In *Othello*, Shakespeare thought of 'motive' as a *force* – 'a moving or exciting cause', rather than a reason for action. In ordinary discourse the word 'motive' covers both meanings – a force and a reason. Enquiries about motive ordinarily mean that we are dealing with a human being rather than a mechanical object. We do not ask what the motive of a car might be. Furthermore, an enquiry about motive assumes that choice is within the capacity of individuals. If we ask about a person's motive for living, we assume that he is continuing at his own choice.

Shakespeare's idiosyncratic use of motive as force has become the rule in psychology where it is assumed that all behaviour is *caused* by forces. Consequently, most concepts in psychology have acquired a pushing or pulling component. Hence the topic of 'motivation', which deals in forces under a variety of names – motives, traits, instincts, drives and needs. While there is an implicit analogy with the concept of force in Newtonian physics, there is also an echo of the metaphorical uses to which we put the term 'force' in everyday life, (e.g. 'I am forced to earn my living'). This metaphorical usage merely implies that one's choice is restricted by circumstances. However, the use of the term in psychology implies, for example, that deprivation of status causes the individual to seek status in the same way as the force of gravity causes a pen to fall if dropped.

An important point about motive-forces in psychology is that they are irredeemably circular. We observe a woman crying and infer a motive-force which is compelling her to do just that. But this is a tautological explanation, not an empirical truth. Of course, it has the added advantage that she cannot be held responsible for her (strategic) behaviour. (It has to be admitted that nowadays popular explanations would refer the causes of her crying to hormones or brain chemicals, but that is another story).

Some psychologists have pointed out that the problem of motivation is a pseudo-problem since explanation of the fact that human beings are active is not necessary. It can be taken that they are and the problem is one of explaining the direction taken by action. When I worked in a psychology department many years ago, there was a proposal put to the faculty to introduce a course on 'motivation'. After acrimonious debate, the proposal was rejected on the grounds that there was nothing to teach since motives are not forces inside the person but *reasons* for human actions which are embedded in their social context. For example, there is an important difference between blinking and winking. While blinking is reactive, individuals have *reasons* for winking or, given the current social environment, not winking.

Like psychologists, managers have eagerly embraced the idea that motives are forces which propel people into action because it appears to provide them with scientific means by which their colleagues may be understood and controlled. If scientists control nature, why can't psychologists and managers control human behaviour?

In ordinary language a need is something which is necessary for some specifiable end, although we rarely nominate the end. So we say: 'I need food', rather than 'I need food if I am to continue to live'. Similarly, I may need an enclosed office if I have to speak confidentially to colleagues. Since to have a need is to have some end in view, one cannot have a need for its own sake. When we talk about needs in this way, there is an understanding that certain needs are more important than others; we think of food as more necessary than an enclosed office. This hints at an order in 'necessary-ness', such that one could rank everything that a person ever needs from the things that are essential to those most easily dispensed with. But this is not acceptable. Things are necessary to the accomplishment of ends strictly in relation to the situation in which people find themselves. Food is essential for maintenance of life, but in some situations antibiotic drugs may be more vital still. Consequently, no fixed hierarchy can be applied to necessity independent of the ends in view.

Maslow's popularity with Australian managers is based on his theory of personality which depends on the notion of a hierarchy of needs. In *Motivation and Personality* he laid it down that people are moved by needs on several levels, which are defined such that no need belonging to a higher level comes into operation until the needs of all inferior levels have been satisfied. From lowest to highest these need levels are: physiological; safety and security; love and belongingness; self-esteem; self-actualisation. At the top of Maslow's hierarchy are notions like self-esteem and self-actualisation which cannot be seen as motive-forces without doing considerable violence to the word 'need'. Everyday talk would regard self-esteem as a desirable state to achieve, whereas Maslow claimed that we are *driven* towards it after certain subordinate goals have been achieved. As an aside, the authors of the Bible did not confuse need as necessity with mere desire.

It is obvious to most people that Maslow's hierarchy is not a true model of human behaviour since there are many instances in which individuals appear to be motivated by needs at the higher levels when the needs they should have at the lower level are not satisfied. A fugitive who is hungry is not forced to eat before attempting to evade his captors. Beethoven engaged in self-actualising behaviour without satisfying his lower levels needs. As a theory of a hierarchy of motive-forces Maslow's has to be rejected. He appears to have recognised this and acknowledged that in practice most people experience a mixture of satisfactions at any one time so the separate levels of needs cannot be taken literally. The main point that emerges from Maslow's theory, however, is that higher order needs are not usually significant until basic needs have been met.

Why, then, is Maslow's theory so popular with Australian managers? I suggest that in management circles this view of human behaviour has been used as a powerful justification for emphasising employees' social relationships and communication skills rather than attending to their demands for more control over their jobs. If social needs are not satisfied – and we might ask whether they can be satisfied in work relationships – there is no point in encouraging employees to pursue personal power, let alone self-actualisation. Similarly, management problems can be defined in terms of 'poor communication' – which they frequently are – while ignoring the substantive content of the communications.

Most management textbooks written after 1950 emphasise the importance of social needs and it is hard to quarrel with writers who profess care and concern for the social well-being of working people. Indeed, it is churlish to suggest that a sleight of hand may be at work and that Maslow's theory has been brilliantly used as a servant of power by allowing managers to direct resources to training in interpersonal skills and personality assessment rather than job enrichment.

Maslow's theory of motivation was entertainingly presented to Australian managers by my colleague at Macquarie University, John Hunt, who was one of the most influential academic trainers in the 1970s. In 1980 he accepted a professorship at the London Business School and by the late 1990s his enthusiasm for Maslow had not waned, as I discovered when we taught together in Germany. He acknowledged the logical and empirical deficiencies of Maslow's hierarchy: 'We have little data to support the concept of a hierarchy of needs in which lower order needs are satisfied before higher (hierarchically) order needs. However, while need hierarchies may be difficult to accept, there is a great deal of data on the relevance of these needs or ends or goals for individuals working in organisations . . .'[1]

The important issue, however, is not whether Maslow's theory is popular but whether it is adequate. The best support for Maslow's theory comes from studies which suggest that if we decrease hierarchical control we will obtain what Maslow calls self-actualising behaviour. This should not surprise us since Maslow's theory was derived from observations of behaviour in social organisations. So studies which appear to support Maslow involve us in circularity. Since his studies are based on the observation of people in social organisations and the ways in which individuals and groups build social structures to provide for their needs and desires, and since hierarchical status predicts satisfaction with needs, studies which confirm Maslow's theory by correlating satisfaction of needs with social status are engaged in the circular process of demonstrating that a theory formulated on the basis of social observation can be supported by observation of the forms of social organisation. We cannot break through to anything that would confirm that Maslow has discovered a hierarchy of motive-forces. He implied that he had discovered a hierarchy of motive-forces which interacts with the social situation in which people find themselves. Yet his hierarchy of needs, which purports to be based in biological structures, is derived solely from a *social* context: the needs themselves are only known from what other people are seen to do, so that the explanation is circular. Indeed this circularity is a feature of *all* personality and motivational perspectives where personality traits and psychological needs are treated as unseen mechanical forces which 'cause' human behaviour.

Managers could promote Maslow's theory as a statement that they should direct their energies towards emancipating colleagues from inferior levels of need, leaving them to work as individuals towards the rather vague higher levels. If, however, we engage in everyday discourse which assumes that individuals are selecting the ends to be achieved and choosing what is necessary for their accomplishments according to their circumstances, we must conclude that they are working with a fluid value-structure: what is vital today may be of no moment tomorrow. Maslow converts this into a fixed hierarchy, which is untenable, and admits needs as mechanical forces. I do not know whether the managers and trainers who promote his theory follow him in this policy. Given the popularity of psychometric testing, where the assumption of force is explicit, it seems likely that they do.

The debate between Drucker and Maslow is part of a wider debate between managing by performance and managing by personality. What is at issue is the role of psychology in management and the degree to which managers want to become psychologists. Drucker argued that management is a practice and that managers are judged and judge others on the basis of objective performance. Maslow argued that management is a form of the human encounter which requires psychological insight into the personality and motives of others. Maslow was not alone and had an army of motivational psychologists to support him, including David McClelland, Frederick Herzberg and other psychologists who became famous, rich and surprisingly influential in the cut-throat business of management.

Psychology generally, and Maslow specifically, have failed to solve the problem of motivation. Considering motive as a force has been a failure because it turns out to be either circular or a metaphor for purpose. This did not bother David McClelland who once declared that his favourite motive – need-achievement – is the 'mental virus' which causes people to become entrepreneurs. Apparently it is the need-power virus that causes other people to become managers. Motives, according to McClelland, are learned. In *The Achieving Society* he argued that the need to achieve is a motive which is absorbed from subtle aspects of parental training, including an emphasis on aspiration, independence, self-reliance and achievement. But what can be learned can be unlearned of forgotten, so motives and the notion of personality they support become highly volatile concepts. McClelland's concept of motive trades, like Maslow's, on human purposiveness and does not really accord with the idea of a force or trait. To pursue material success as an entrepreneur in American society is more like a reasonable choice of means to secure success than a fixed personality disposition. Furthermore, it is probable that the same people who become entrepreneurs would seek success in other walks of life, regardless of the manner in which their parents behaved towards them. There is also the problem of those brought up in the ethos prescribed for prospective entrepreneurs who become something quite different, managers for example. The idea that motives are learned compelled McClelland to deny that personality is a matter of fixed traits that cut across rational behaviour. He was obliged to demonstrate that the achievement motive is anything more than ordinary rational, purposive behaviour. To achieve this, he needed to demonstrate that this motive springs from the person in spite of the environment, and his very assumption that it is learned prevented such a demonstration.

Like Maslow's, McClelland's theory of motivation became popular in the 1960s with managers when it was reported that they too were motivated by the achievement virus. Only later were they re-diagnosed as suffering from a power virus. Incidentally, McClelland and other 'need' theorists contravene a basic rule of English grammar, which stipulates that if a noun is used adjectivally it must precede the noun it qualifies and not the other way round. So we find McClelland describing ambition as 'need achievement' or 'n Ach' instead of achievement need; power seeking is 'need power' or 'n Pow'; sociability is 'need affiliation' or 'n Aff'. Mercifully, he doesn't commit them to a hierarchy of viruses.

Polish sociologist Stanislav Andreski had great fun with the notion of 'need'. To prove to himself that he too could make pseudo-scientific discoveries and that his opposition to psychologists was not motivated by impotent envy, he sent a letter to a sociological journal. In his witty book, *Social Sciences as Sorcery*, he quoted a sample of his paper and invited the reader to guess what he meant by 'n Bam':

'In connection with David McClelland's article it might be relevant to report that the preliminary results of our research project into the encoding processes in communication flow indicate that (owing to their multiplex permutations) it is difficult to ascertain direct correlates of 'n Aff'. On the other hand when on the encephalogram 'dy' divided by 'dx' is less than '0', 'n Ach' attains a significantly high positive correlation with 'n Bam', notwithstanding the partially stochastic nature of the connection between these two variables.'

After the publication of this letter Andreski was approached by several industrial research organisations who offered cooperation. After inviting his readers to decipher what his letter actually said, he offered the following translation:

'Owing to the waywardness of human nature it is difficult to find out why people join a given group, but observation of how people speak and write clearly suggests that, when the brain is slowing down, a desire to achieve often gives rise to a need to bamboozle.'[2]

Andreski argued that the use of the letter 'n' helps authors cash in on the prestige of mathematics, which seems to be the only reason for replacing 'desire' with 'need' or 'n'. As any rational person knows, people often desire what they do not need, and what may even do them harm (such as excessive food), while needing what they do not desire (such as constructive criticism).

Apart from Maslow and McClelland, the most influential theorist of motivation in Australian management was Frederick Herzberg who is remembered for his claim that money is not a motivator. When it was learned that he was charging thousands of dollars for a lecture and was challenged by a member of his audience to defend his theory of motivation, his legendary reply was: 'Hell, I didn't say that money doesn't matter.'

In the late 1950s Herzberg and his colleagues reviewed motivational research spanning fifty years and 28,000 employees. The most frequently mentioned sources of job satisfaction were the 'social aspects of the job', a term which the authors used to refer to all job contacts made by employees with their colleagues.

The second most frequently mentioned factor was the employees' interactions with their supervisors. But it was not social interaction in any general sense that is satisfying to an individual, but specific kinds of outcomes, such as having power over or being liked by others. Herzberg concluded that satisfied employees are realistic about their lives and goals, more flexible, better adjusted people who have the capacity to overcome the effects of poor environments. Dissatisfied employees, on the other hand, are often rigid, inflexible, unrealistic in their choice of goals, unable to overcome problems, and generally unhappy.

With his 1968 book, *Work and the Nature of Man*, Herzberg hit the management jackpot and toured the conference circuit as a guru for the next decade. In 1995 the International Press announced that this book was one of the ten most influential books in management in the twentieth century.

Herzberg began with the assumption that humans have animalistic and achievement needs. The achievement needs are like Maslow's growth needs and are concerned with the uniquely human desire to grow psychologically. The animalistic needs are concerned with the job environment and the achievement needs with the content of the job. He noted that employees responded differently to questions about what they liked and disliked about their jobs. So he asked 200 engineers and accountants in Pittsburgh to recall 'critical incidents' when they had felt 'exceptionally good' or 'exceptionally bad' about their jobs. He found that incidents relating to 'good' periods tended to refer to the content of the work itself, while those relating to 'bad' periods were mainly concerned with the context in which work was performed. He therefore separated 'motivating' factors which lead to job satisfaction from 'hygiene' factors which prevent dissatisfaction but do not promote satisfaction. Factors involved in job content – achievement, recognition, challenge, responsibility and advancement – are strong determinants of satisfaction. Factors involved in job dissatisfaction, however, are rarely involved in events that led to positive job attitudes. Also, unlike the satisfiers, the dissatisfiers consistently produced short-term changes in job attitudes. The major dissatisfiers are company policy and administration, supervision, salary, interpersonal relationships and working conditions. Since the dissatisfiers describe the environment and serve primarily to prevent job dissatisfaction while having little effect on positive job attitudes, Herzberg named them 'hygiene' factors. The satisfiers were named 'motivators' since they are effective in motivating people to superior effort. It would follow that the way to motivate working people is through job enrichment: challenging work for which employees assume responsibility. Herzberg noted, however, that managers usually try to bribe employees with hygiene factors, such as incentive schemes and fringe benefits. What is needed is more emphasis on good, old-fashioned Puritan virtues, notably hard work, responsibility and achievement.

Herzberg also applied his theory to the vexed field of mental health. Mental illness is not the mere absence of mental health. Nor is mental health the mere absence of mental illness. Mental health and illness are two separate dimensions representing approach behaviour (mental health) and avoidance behaviour (mental illness). Combining his interest in work motivation with mental health, he asserted that employees who seek to obtain satisfactions from material rewards (rather than from sources approved by managers) are not only 'sick', 'unhealthy' and 'maladjusted', but 'mentally ill', 'neurotic' and 'patholo-gical' as well. He argued that satisfaction with material rewards (which may reduce deprivation) indicates emotional immaturity. Employees who are deprived in some physical or financial way are more likely to suffer emotional problems, but if the source of deprivation is removed (say pay them more) they are still likely to have emotional problems unless they develop interests in 'higher order' factors, such as achievement, challenge and responsibility. Obviously employees at the bottom of organisational hierarchies are more likely to be denied access to challenging jobs and their concern with material rewards would seem reasonable. According to Herzberg, however, they are neurotic.

Throughout the 1970s it was a form of sport for psychologists to criticise Herzberg's theory. It is easily done. By relying on a story-telling method he is vulnerable to the charge that the differences between stated sources of satisfaction and dissatisfaction stem from defensive processes. People are more likely to attribute the causes of satisfaction to their own achievements while attributing their dissatisfaction to factors in their environment. When researchers used methods other than the critical-incident story-telling approach, Herzberg's results were not confirmed. Despite, or because of, academic criticism Herzberg's influence on Australian management increased throughout the 1970s. His theory was appropriated by people interested in job enrichment and the semi-autonomous work group movement in Scandinavia. If managers are serious in their desire to maximise job satisfaction at the workplace, it followed from Herzberg's theory that they should eliminate sources of job dissatisfaction from the work environment and increase possibilities for job enrichment by redesigning jobs to promote personal challenge and responsibility. But Herzberg was adamant that job enrichment must be based on an 'individual' psychology of motivation (popular in America and based on a Protestant Ethic ideology) and not on the 'group' psychology (popular in Scandinavia and widely but erroneously associated with socialism).

Herzberg's comparison between individual and group psychology is crucial to an understanding of the confusions that developed in Australian management in the 1970s and led to the rejection of job enrichment programs that were based on the Scandinavian model. By the 1980s Australian managers had, with Herzberg's help, buried the Scandinavian approach and were dancing with psychologists and consultants who were promoting Japanese ideas. Australian managers preferred Herzberg's 'individual' psychology, with its emphasis on individual achievement, personal responsibility and recognition for personal achievement, to the Scandinavian emphasis on group behaviour. These concepts are consistent with the Protestant Ethic, which is an appropriate ideology for a red-blooded American psychologist like Herzberg who simply ignored power relationships in favour of personal motives.

Herzberg argued that the European emphasis on worker participation and industrial democracy reflects ideological bias of the left. His own defence of rampant individualism presumably reflected ideological bias of the right, although he did not say so. And so we appear to be faced with an ideological impasse. Scandinavian psychologists argued that while managers gain their power and satisfactions from their job and higher-order motives, blue-collar workers gain their power and satisfactions through the group. Herzberg, however, feared the domination of the individual by the group and directed his attention to the virtues of individual achievement and personal responsibility, which may be valid for managers but sentences blue-collar workers to impotence.

In 1974 when Herzberg was treading the boards at management conferences David Jenkins published a critique of Herzberg and his version of job enrichment. *Job Power* had little influence on Australian managers who preferred the motivation-hygiene gospel preached by the globe-trotting missionary. Though delivered with wit and energy, Herzberg's message became increasingly shrill and dogmatic. When members of his audiences, especially Europeans, suggested that human motivation is more complex than he indicated, the guru frequently implied

that research undertaken since his own had been quite unnecessary and replied: 'You got an expert's answer'. When confronted
with studies which showed that when faced with boring and
repetitive work workers view high pay and good physical
working conditions as the only sources of satisfaction, which
is not supposed to happen according to his theory, Herzberg
retreated to the position that such people are neurotic.

Herzberg's version of job enrichment yields only limited
changes since the way in which the jobs are enriched is decided,
not by workers, but imposed without group discussion by the
external job enrichment experts, or human resource managers.
He was against group action and participation in decision-making
processes and was worried that workers would participate beyond
their level of competence. Jenkins is surely right when he argued
that Herzberg's popularity among American (and Australian)
managers depended on his method's very limited objectives.
While it goes some way toward satisfying some employees, it
does not alter prevailing power relationships. After all, Herzberg
had said that the authoritarian pattern of American industry
will continue 'despite the propaganda for a more democratic
way of life.' And telling managers that money is not a motivator
must have come as a pleasant surprise to those who regarded
wages as a cost to be minimised.

Jenkins noted the lack of progress in job enrichment in
America despite Herzberg's popularity and he asked why it should
be that, after such a promising start, managers and employees
had been overtaken by feelings of apathy about its prospects.
The same was said of job enrichment and worker participation
in Australia, by Russell Lansbury for example.[3] In stark contrast,
Scandinavian psychologists were reporting significant progress
with semi-autonomous work groups in which employees were
given and responded positively to increased levels of control over
their jobs. Yet the degree of interest in the US in job enrichment

through increased job control was close to zero. Jenkins pointed out that this apathy was not confined to managers, who might be expected to resist changes in relative power structures, but was also widespread among trade union officials, social scientists and social commentators generally.

It was left to the Scandinavians to take the lead in job enrichment and to face the problems of power and authority relationships. One of the leading exponents in this area was Einar Thorsrud whose work at Nobo Fabrikker and Norsk Hydro paved the way for 'task force' type operations in Sweden, notably at the Volvo and Saab factories. Thorsrud, with help from the Tavistock Institute in London and Australia's Fred Emery, reorganised work practices to such an extent that through the establishment of groups with common goals, power relationships were improved. Jenkins noted that it is significant that Thorsrud's basic assumptions of human motivation were similar to Herzberg's. Yet Herzberg, who was against group actions of this type, was not made to confront the problems of power and authority generated by such action, such as the doubts raised by job enrichment programmes about the unwarranted size of middle management. For Herzberg each individual is to be dealt with individually.

Herzberg disapproved of the Scandinavian experiments and their major disadvantage – group tyranny. He was concerned about the individual and not the group member per se, assuming that individuals can be subtracted from their social milieu, which is impossible. He made outlandish claims about fundamental differences between theories which emphasise *personal* responsibility (like his) and others which do not. He argued that employee commitment to groups, far from being a source of power for them, robs them of their individuality. Not only is this not supported empirically, it is not even a feature of Scandinavian theory. Rather, it is consistent with a pervasive Protestant

Ethic ideology which Herzberg scarcely bothered to conceal. When researchers compared work experiences on the production lines of Sweden and Detroit, there was no evidence that the Swedes were tyrannised by the group and plenty of evidence that they were healthier, more productive and motivated to work. The wide gap between American and Scandinavian ideas about job enrichment was illuminated during a seminar at which Thorsrud and Herzberg were present. Jenkins reported that Herzberg was expressing his gloomy views on the dangers of worker participation and Thorsrud replied that he (Herzberg) was against participation for the very reasons the Scandinavians were in favour of it – one doesn't know where it will stop.

By removing the emphasis from problems of material and financial deprivation to personal inadequacies and emotional immaturity, Herzberg's theory contradicted the considerable evidence which showed that it is *rational* for blue-collar workers to be concerned with their physical, material and financial well-being. If managers believe that joining a trade union or negotiating for higher wages and better working conditions is indicative of incipient madness or blatant irrationality, they are following in the footsteps of one of the most influential industrial psychologists of the twentieth century. Such a fact might be comical if it occurred only in caricature. Unfortunately, the reality is that many Australian managers believed it. One consequence was that Scandinavian experiments were routinely dismissed in the late 1970s as misguided, impractical and ideologically unsound.

There were some notable exceptions, however. A handful of companies encouraged participation and involvement by employees on the shop-floor. These programmes included the election by work groups of their own supervisors, the restructuring of jobs to provide workers with greater opportunities to exercise choice and initiative, and the creation of self-managing work groups which managed their own work schedules and decided how tasks should be shared and performed. The underlying objective of these programmes was to introduce 'management from below' to replace the traditional approach of 'rule from above'. Fred Emery's experience at the Tavistock Institute of Human Relations in England and his work with the Scandinavian industrial democracy projects influenced much local activity in this field. The introduction of semi-autonomous work groups at CSR Limited, for example, required an increase in the range of workers' skills, as was the case with the self-managing work groups in Pacific Can Company.

When, in 1979, I went to Sweden to study the semi-autonomous work groups at Volvo and Saab, the news from Australia was that I was wasting my time because the heady days of 'industrial democracy', championed in Don Dunstan's state of South Australia, were over. On my return to Australia the refrain from managers was: 'You can't transplant Sweden to Australia.' True enough, but having rejected the possibility of borrowing ideas from one country, Australian managers began their long love affair with another – Japan.

In 1982 *International Management* published a cover story headed, 'Where have all the management gurus gone?'[4] The authors lamented the fact that there were no new faces in the gallery of management gurus. Since psychologists entered the field of management in the 1950s and 1960s, there have been no writers to rival Herzberg, McGregor or Maslow. The authors conceded that of all the influential management scribes only Drucker was still producing original and stimulating material. Drucker himself conceded that the new management gurus are yet to be discovered. Those with the potential to achieve eminent status were busy writing books telling people how to make money out of nuclear war or how to profit from world starvation.

However, in the early 1980s there were many Australian managers who believed that a new guru had emerged who could explain the unexplainable: the workings of the Japanese mind. William G Ouchi joined the long list of management professors who attempted to understand the 'Japanese miracle' and educate local managers in the ways of the Japanese. At a time when Japanese productivity was the highest in the world, it is hardly surprising that American and Australian managers responded favourably to an author who offered to lead them from the halcyon days of American human relations to a new era of Japanese-style paternalism. The Japanese model promised to replace obsessions with job satisfaction and sociability with concerns for productivity and adaptation to a new era of 'consumer freedom'. The gurus of the 1950s and 1960s had, with the notable exception of Drucker, passed into history precisely because the world's economic and social developments had rendered their ideas impotent.

Sometime during the 1970s the world entered a new and turbulent period. Most of the amazing changes in the world economy had been predicted twenty-five years earlier. The 1950s and 1960s were decades of considerable growth but the developments were largely the result of the application of discoveries made in the Second World War and shortly thereafter. Management writers who achieved fame with motivational theories offered few, if any, insights that had not been developed before the depression of the 1930s. Indeed, the advocates of worker participation, who had their brief moment of glory in the mid-1970s, merely restated arguments rehearsed in the early years of the century. The much publicised achievements of the Volvo and Saab plants in Sweden were, as we have seen, the result of ideas and practices adopted in General Motors and other American companies in the war when shortages of supervisors and engineers forced radical changes to management assumptions and practices.

By the early 1980s, however, it had become obvious to many managers that concerns for and improvements to employees' levels of job satisfaction had not resulted in improvements in productivity, absenteeism or industrial conflict. Furthermore, the short-lived movement for worker participation threatened to put more power into the hands of trade unionists at a time when citizens of the developed countries were telling opinion polls that union officials should have less power. Oddly enough, union officials themselves allowed the participation movement to die without a whimper. Some in union officialdom believed that worker participation would lead to a combination of employers and unionists against consumers at a time when consumers were demanding more freedom. Others were concerned it would compromise the power of trade unions, and even render them irrelevant. Thus it appeared that a new management guru would have to address a different set of problems and develop a radically different approach to management. Australian managers had moved into an era of discontinuity and they had to learn how to manage in turbulent times. Apart from Drucker's new books, they could no longer rely on Maslow, McClelland and Herzberg. The need of affiliation had been replaced by a 'new individualism' which managers found increasingly difficult to live with.

Then along came William Ouchi who advised managers to prepare for the new era of productivity by learning from those great producers – the Japanese. His best-selling book *Theory Z* purported to show how American managers could meet the Japanese challenge. He argued that companies which resemble the large Japanese organisations could significantly increase employee satisfaction and productivity because they were homogeneous and collectivistic and allowed individual behaviours to mesh intimately. By comparison, Ouchi argued, American organisations were heterogeneous and individualistic which meant that people linked tenuously to one another. He brought a smile to readers when he claimed that American organisations which had, in the 1980s, evolved 'Japanese' form included IBM, Procter and Gamble, Hewlett-Packard, Eastman Kodak, and were therefore to be emulated. Acknowledging McGregor's Theory Y, Ouchi referred to these 'American/Japanese' organisations as Type Z As we have seen, Theory Y was more a programme than a theory and McGregor used it to argue for participative management and the decentralisation of organisational power. In the early1960s this was radical thinking. By the 1970s it was all the rage until Australian managers decided to waltz with the Japanese. And along came Ouchi to teach them how to dance.

Ouchi believed that Z organisations are based on clans rather than hierarchies. Clans succeed when teamwork replaces individual performance. And because of the relative absence of bureaucratic controls, individuals report a higher sense of personal autonomy, which makes them work with more enthusiasm than their counterparts in Western organisations. Before proceeding, a few comments about the consequences of *not* working with enthusiasm are in order.

Ouchi's arguments applied to about one-third of employed males and no females in Japan. For those who entered the doors of large Japanese companies as employees, security and prosperity were guaranteed so long as work was performed willingly and efficiently. For those who were not accepted by the large companies life was much harder. There were thousands of small backyard businesses which supplied their products to one large organisation and where conditions of work were far worse than the most deprived industrial plants in Australia. Presumably, feelings of autonomy were less pronounced among those who had been unable to cope with the enormous pressures to gain admission to the elite business corporations and government agencies. While Ouchi provided a general description of the workings of Japanese society, he failed to analyse the relationship between social authority and organisational authority. Indeed the word 'authority' does not appear in his index. Rather, he followed the American tendency to explain authority relationships in terms of *trust*. For example, he believed that the authoritarian system of job placement in Japan, in which students from elite universities are selected for work in elite companies, is based on trust. So, for Ouchi, the first lesson of Theory Z is trust, and productivity and trust go hand in hand, 'strange as that may seem.' Not strange at all because with trust and productivity go power and authority. And it is all too easy to explain employee obedience by an appeal to feelings of intimacy and trust and ignore the fact that the penalties for disobedience and distrust are very severe indeed. It may be that feelings of autonomy make the Japanese work enthusiastically. Alternatively, feelings of autonomy may be rationalisations which enable the Japanese to accept the limits to their autonomy which result from social conditions that support life-time employment (in the large companies and government departments) and provide significant rewards to those who conform to the system.

Ouchi acknowledged the weaknesses of the clan model: xenophobia, overweening conformity and conservatism, racism, sexism, loss of professionalism. But although Theory Z is based on trust, mutual obligation, consensus and harmony, Ouchi failed to address the crucial issues of conflict, tensions and pressures which characterise the daily life of Japanese employees and the bitter factional fighting which consume most Japanese managers. Drucker had warned his American readers that Japanese business life is a saga of unremitting guerrilla warfare.[5] Where the foreigner sees close cooperation between government and business, the Japanese managers see government bureaucrats meddling and dictating to them, a constant tug-of-war between and within organisations. In this respect, Ouchi was indeed a foreigner. He saw trust, harmony and consensus where others saw a finely balanced system of power relationships. He was right to extol the virtues of trust and intimacy, since part of the Japanese success story of the 1980s was based on the willingness of the various parties to establish areas of common concern. He was also right in pointing out that work organisations are profoundly shaped by the social environment in which they operate. But this insight was set aside when Theory Z was born. By imposing a personal model of harmony and consensus upon the Japanese experience he misunderstood its power relationships.

With little theory to guide Theory Z most of Ouchi's book was devoted to 'how to' issues. (This, according to Drucker, disqualified him from guru status). But there is little in Ouchi's 'how to' steps that cannot be found in books on organisational development that were popular in the 1950s. These books rarely face the problem of how to bring together individuals whose main reason for working is economic. As Australian employees' involvement with work organisations is primarily calculative the application of Theory Z, which required a stronger degree of moralistic involvement than has ever been achieved in this country, was unlikely to succeed.

Ouchi's star has faded and he is rarely mentioned today. Similarly, the glories of Japan have faded into history and managers today are more concerned to understand China and India, although they are reluctant to look to those countries for management models. Ouchi marched to the tune of those naïve psychologists who claimed that the adversarial relationships between American managers and workers should be replaced by mutual trust. He offered benevolent paternalism at a time when managers were witnessing the beginning of the end of 'organisation man'. Ouchi's brief success signalled the end of an era. Theory Z was a pendant to McGregor's psychology of 1960. He continued, and perhaps concluded, the tradition of human relations thinkers who have survived far longer than many would have predicted.

5

The Personality Cult

Psychological tests: Putting the litmus paper of the psyche into the snake oil of tyrants; widely used by managers to control other managers; a self-destructive enterprise if ever there was one.

Personologists and their colleagues in the personality testing industry may disagree about their favourite tools but they agree with the following assumptions about human behaviour. Social phenomena – crime, politics, sexuality, smoking, mental illness – are to be understood as the sum of the personalities of individuals. Although they are not objects personality traits can be treated as if they are properties in the brain. The properties can be measured on a scale so that individuals can be ranked according to the amounts of the properties they possess. General population norms can be established so that 'normality' and 'abnormality' can be determined. Deviations from normality – abnormalities – can be treated as medical or psychological problems for which individuals should be 'treated'. The medicalised properties can be considered as caused by events in the brains of abnormal individuals and associated with the brain's biochemistry. Individual behaviour can be treated as if it is caused by the interaction of genetic and environmental forces. It is therefore important to measure personality since it is assumed that behaviour is caused by traits which are located inside individuals. The traits are assumed to be rigid, relatively unchanging 'things' that can be measured indirectly through psychometric tests. It is further assumed that they do not vary much from week to week.

Personality traits are measured by adding individuals' answers to questions which purport to assess behavioural themes and by which individuals are compared to others in a group. Particular traits are then reduced to personality factors which are classification systems, even though they are treated as inner causes of behaviour. So a person works hard because of 'ambition' or gains the support of others because of 'sociability'. Yet all that is available by way of evidence is the behaviour from which the trait was inferred.

The popularity of personality tests suggests that psychomanagers do not regard performance as the ultimate test of management. Or to put it another way, the traditional test of management has been compromised by psychomanagers and personologists since personality is, according to empirical evidence spanning more than half a century, unrelated to work performance. These findings, endlessly replicated, should lead to the rational conclusion that personality tests can make no contribution to management. But the opposite, irrational conclusion prevails.

Despite the logical and empirical problems that dominate the field, psychomanagers continue to pay psychologists to measure personality traits, and subject individuals to psychometric tests in the belief, or hope, that the elusive relationship between performance and personality will be found. Some psychomanagers accept the lack of relationship between personality and performance but argue that psychometric tests enable them to make decisions about the 'fit' between individual and organisation. But since personality and performance are unrelated, decisions about 'organisational fit' are based on prejudices, stereotypes and caricatures. One still hears psychomanagers claim that extraverts make better salespeople than do introverts, individuals with low anxiety are more productive than those with high anxiety, high levels of emotional intelligence predict success in management, and so on. There is no empirical evidence to support any of these assumptions.

Defenders of psychometric tests have claimed that knowing something about another person's personality enables managers to do their job more effectively. The assumption is that since personality determines performance managers can motivate their subordinates by reducing them to specific personality traits and applying motivational techniques thereto. But personality does not 'determine' performance, wholly or partly. Personality traits do not 'exist' in the way in which work performance 'exists'. Traits are inferences from behaviour and they do not cause behaviour. Psychomanagers are not content to work with behaviour however. They seek the keys to the kingdom of the psyche.

The extraordinary appeal of inner causes of behaviour must be due to more than illiteracy, illogic or irresponsibility. B F Skinner fought for decades against the seductive power of inner causes of behaviour. 'I suggest that it has the appeal of the arcane, the occult, the hermetic, the magical – those mysteries which have held so important a position in the history of human thought. It is the appeal of an apparently inexplicable power, in a world which seems to lie beyond the senses and the reach of reason. It is the appeal still enjoyed by astrology, numerology, parapsychology and psychical research.'[1]

Personality testers rely on evidence – personal, anecdotal, empirical – to conclude that the theory that personality predicts performance is valid. However, all empirical hypotheses are conjectural in the sense that we shall never be able to have absolute confidence that they are true, even if most of us would agree to accept some conjectures as more credible than others. While no number of black ravens could verify the claim that all are black, a single raven that is not black can falsify the hypothesis. The strength of a *scientific* theory, therefore, rests on its ability to withstand criticism.

The theory that personality predicts management performance has been repeatedly falsified by hundreds of studies over a period exceeding fifty years. The history of failure has been so pronounced that personality trait theory should be regarded as a degenerated research programme. But that would be to underestimate the power of bad science and vested interests. Indeed, personality testing in industry and government has never been more popular. In the US more than 40 percent of large companies spend $400 million dollars each year on psychometric testing. In the UK the *Association of Graduate Recruiters* reported that 92 percent of employers surveyed in 2007 considered psychometric testing an important tool for recruitment. The authors of a recent management textbook state: 'it appears that the use of these (personality) tests for recruitment purposes in Australian organisations is increasing, despite criticism of them as unreliable and unethical.' Helen De Cicri and Robin Kramar quote a survey of 8000 people in which 44 percent regarded psychometric tests as 'too invasive with regard to personal facts and details', which they are. Yet a survey of Australian human resource managers showed that 69 percent believe that personality tests are valuable tools which can be used to improve performance.[2]

Personality testing is big business. Professional journals include testimonials from consultants and managers who parade their paeans proudly. Paeans are justified when these songs of joy are linked to triumphant outcomes otherwise the songs are empty and the victory pyrrhic. Sadly, a review of the personality testing industry leads to the undeniable conclusion that the triumph is based on the widespread, but false, belief that personality test scores predict individual performance. If they did one could have no empirical objection to them, although one might still object to their use with unwilling subjects on moral grounds. But personality test scores do not predict performance, as countless scholars have pointed out for decades.

Reviewers of personality testing have been insisting for half a century that improvements are needed in the reliability and validity of personality tests. The general conclusion is that improvements are needed not only in the reliability and validity of personality tests but also in their theoretical underpinnings and the criteria against which they are validated. Popular tests are invalid indicators of what they purport to measure, infringe on the individual's right to privacy, and foster unethical management practices. No surprises here since this is a familiar refrain. It is a disheartening experience to hear apologists agree that the old popular tests were unreliable and invalid, but assure us that new tests have overcome earlier problems. It is a discreditable business when psychologists tell clients that their tests can predict behaviour while admitting that there are no relevant validation studies. Which personalities are desirable and which are undesirable? We cannot know.

Personologists claim that the acquisition of various skills is influenced by personality traits. This claim still awaits empirical evidence to support it. And it is difficult to see how it could ever find such support given the theoretical nature of traits and the vast discrepancy between what people say and what they do. Personality traits are *abstractions* so they cannot cause anyone to do anything. How then did testers convince people that personality traits exist and can be measured? Since many personologists treat traits as 'mental forces' they needed to convince people that they are populated by invisible powers. A linguistic trick was needed and it has been prosecuted with considerable success.

The trick is based on the practice of turning verbs and adverbs into abstract nouns and *reifying* them, i.e., treating the abstract nouns as if they are concrete nouns. Concrete nouns refer to such things as tables; abstract nouns do not refer to things, which is why they are called 'abstract'. So the verb 'think' became the abstract noun 'thought', 'feel' became 'feeling', 'intelligently' became 'intelligence', 'create' became 'creativity', 'imagine' became 'imagination', 'depressed' became 'depression', and so on. If an abstract noun, say 'thought', is treated as a concrete noun a place has to be found to house it. The house is either another abstraction called 'mind' (from the verb 'to mind'), or a concrete entity – brain – although logic demands that an abstraction cannot be located anywhere. In this way people are populated with abstractions – thoughts, feelings, values, intelligences (cognitive, emotional, spiritual, moral) and minds. While it is true that we think, feel, value, act intelligently (sometimes), and mind (as in 'mind the step'), it is not true that we have 'things' called thoughts, feelings, values, intelligences or minds.

Reifying abstract nouns allows, say, management performance to be explained by 'pride' or 'ambition' although it is impossible to determine which trait is the cause of performance. Used thus, reification is a powerful political tool because it enables psychomanagers to identify people whose personalities don't 'fit' or who lack a 'well-rounded personality'. In extreme cases it enables them to conclude that their colleagues are suffering from a 'personality disorder'.

Should there be any doubt about the efficacy of this programme, there is the psychiatric bible, *Diagnostic and Statistical Manual of Mental Disorders,* to support those psychomanagers who label non-conformists and troublemakers as 'personality disordered'. *DSM* (i.e. the American Psychiatric Association) defines personality disorder as an enduring pattern of inner experience and behaviour that deviates markedly from the expectations of the individual's culture. The authors admit that assessment can also be complicated by the fact that the characteristics that define a personality disorder may not be considered problematic by the individual. Indeed! This definition enables people to be discriminated against on the spurious grounds that their 'inner experience' (as allegedly revealed through personality tests) or behaviour (as judged by, sometimes hostile, others) deviates markedly from the expectations of the society or group in which they live. But who judges 'deviation', 'markedly', and 'expectations'?

Furthermore, personology is based on a tautology. When we are told that a person acts from a trait which, at the time of acting, is the dominant one, we are in the grip of tautology. Traits cannot be observed so they are inferred from observations of behaviour, including answers to test questions. The 'aggression' trait is an inference from the observation that a particular person frequently acts aggressively. The circularity of reasoning is obvious. How do we know that a person has an 'aggression' trait? He has an 'aggression' trait because he acts aggressively. Why does he act aggressively? He acts aggressively because he has an 'aggression' trait, or an aggressive personality.

It is axiomatic that when we make a claim of the form x (aggression) causes y (aggressive behaviour), x and y must be *separately* identifiable. We can identify aggressive behaviour (y) but no one has ever observed an aggression trait (x). So when we are told that a person acts from the trait which, at the time of acting, is the dominant one, the statement is tautological. It is logically impossible that a person could 'possess' a dominant trait and yet be driven into action by a subordinate trait. If the subordinate trait is 'causing' the behaviour, it is by definition the dominant trait. Personality trait psychology, therefore, is based on a tautology. And from a tautology one cannot deduce a statement about the empirical world: tautologies have tautological consequences. One cannot, for example, deduce from the tautology 'what will be, will be', that effort is worthless. Similarly, one cannot deduce from the tautology that one acts from a dominant trait that there are any such traits. Personality trait psychology is trapped in circularity.

There is an escape route for those who want to assess behavioural trends but do not wish to populate the individual with personality traits. Answers to personality tests can be treated as communications about the hypothetical situations invented by test designers, including the testing environment itself. Needless to say, the logic of the testing situation is conveniently ignored by testers who assume that subjects answer questionnaire items honestly and thereby reveal something about their habitual patterns of behaviour. Testers assume that measured patterns of behaviour are triggered by social situations similar to those described in questionnaires. This chain of reasoning is weak at every link since there is no justification for the view that behaviour across time and social situations is consistent. Behaviour, as everyone knows, varies according to the situation in which one finds oneself. The results of personality tests are communications not traits, self-reports not needs, and they are particularly responsive to the demands of one's social situation.

Psychologists cannot know another person's inner experiences: all they can know are communications about them. Personality tests cannot measure inner experiences: they measure honest and dishonest communications. Since many people are required to undergo personality testing against their will, some communicate dishonestly. Indeed, faking personality tests is so widespread and so easy to accomplish that it is surprising that the results are taken seriously. There have been numerous demonstrations that faking can be successful. And the claim that personality tests contain lie scales which can identify fakers is risible.

In the 1950s, William Whyte made fools of personality testers when he wrote an appendix to his best-selling book called 'How to Cheat on Personality Tests'.[3] Legions of people followed his sensible advice. The important thing to recognise is that one doesn't win a good score, one avoids a bad one. What a bad score is depends on the subjective impressions of the tester. Safety lies in getting a score somewhere between the fortieth and sixtieth percentiles, which is to say, one should try to answer like every-body else is supposed to answer. Now this is not always easy to judge so, when in doubt, testees should follow two rules: when asked for views about the world, give the most conventional, pedestrian answer possible; to settle on the best answer to any question, repeat:

(a) I loved my father and my mother, but my father a little bit more;
(b) I like things pretty well the way they are;
(c) I never worry much about anything;
(d) I don't care for books or music much;
(e) I love my wife (husband/partner) and children;
(f) I don't let them get in the way of company work.

When answering personality tests one should stay in char-acter, pretend to support the values of the tester, avoid extreme positions, answer conservatively, and choose a convenient neurosis. One should be very careful when answering such ques-tions as 'I often get pink spots all over'. They are by-products of efforts to screen 'mentally ill' people and were designed by psychologists working in mental institutions. Managers have no business asking these questions, but they do. If asked about spiders or relationships with parents one should remain consistent and as much in character as possible. A few mild neuroses conceded here and there won't yield a bad score, and in conceding neuroses one should know that the biggest margin for error is to err on the side of being 'manic', i.e., too energetic and active.

After reviewing more than half a century's research on personality testing, many scholars have concluded that they cannot under any circumstance advocate the use of personality tests as a basis for making decisions about individual performance. Faced with low validity data, advocates have blamed the adverse results on poor research practices and have used statistical sleight of hand to convince a gullible public of the importance of personality tests. The technical deficiencies of the most widely used tests are well known. For example, the *Humm-Wadsworth Temperament Scale* (HWS) has poor reliabilities, which raises concerns about the accuracy of individual assessments. The popular *Myers-Briggs Temperament Indicator* (MBTI) contradicts the original Jungian ideas on which it is based and studies using the test have neither confirmed the theory nor validated the measure.

Developed in the US in the early 1930s the HWS was known in the 1940s as a 'people-sorting instrument'. 'People-sorters' were early personality tests designed to meet the needs of big business. And they, in turn, became big business. 'People-sorters' first became popular in the 1920s when they were used for dubious purposes, such as screening out political liberals and union sympathisers. In *The Servants of Power* Loren Baritz reported that the HWS was used at Lockheed to identify and remove possible troublemakers from among employment applicants. Another company used personality tests to discover whether applicants' wives dominated their family decisions, because it was believed that such men would be easy to manage and this was just the sort of men the company wanted. The HWS was used to detect such temperaments as autistic, paranoid, epileptoid, depressive, manic, hysteroid, schizoid, cycloid. 'Normal-cycloid' individuals are, it seems, good salespeople while 'normal-autistics' are good accountants. It was assumed that every job had an ideal personality to 'fit' it. The challenge was to find the right cog for the machine.

Isabel Myers, a Philadelphia housewife with no training in psychology, read about the HWS in a 1942 *Reader's Digest* and it changed her life. By entering the people-sorting business Myers believed she could create world peace, or at least make people nicer, and gave birth to her 'baby' – the MBTI. Inspired by an eccentric reading of Carl Jung, Myers developed a test which allegedly measured such traits as 'intuition' and 'feeling'. A few months before her death in 1980 she was toasted by her disciples as 'an intellectual giant' and presented with a necklace with her MBTI score inscribed in gold letters: she was of course 'intuitive' and a 'feeler'.

The MBTI assesses the extent to which individuals have a dominant preference for particular behaviours and ways of thinking. A self-report, forced-choice test, its four 'preference' scales measure extraversion-introversion, sensing-intuiting, thinking-feeling, judging-perceiving. Because of the method of scoring (based on dichotomies) there have been legitimate concerns about the test's psychometric properties and its use in business and academic environments. Several researchers have failed to replicate the MBTI's factor structure and concluded that the naming of the factors is vague and tendentious. Sound empirical investigations of the test are rare and it has been difficult to establish relationships between personality types and organisational factors. It should not be used to 'type' individuals for particular jobs, although it has been used for that purpose. The test contains many transparent items so that it is easily faked.

The MBTI has achieved true cult status. It is now the world's most popular test according to its guardians: more than 2.5 million people take the test in a year. The MBTI is used by 89 of the Fortune 100 companies to 'identify strengths' and 'facilitate teamwork'. Annie Murphy Paul observed that the MBTI has also been embraced by numerous lost souls who experience a revelation (the 'aha reaction') upon learning about psychological type. Their enthusiasm persists despite research showing that as many as three-quarters of testees achieve a different personality type when tested again, and the sixteen types described by the MBTI have no scientific basis whatsoever.

It is easy to see why it appeals to so many people in management, academia, education, counselling and coaching. New age fantasists, lost souls in search of gurus or themselves, narcissists, politically correct relativists, psychologists and their clients who emphasise 'feeling and caring' rather than 'thinking and arguing', have found the MBTI a revelation. 'Original and independent-minded as she was, Isabel Myers managed to create a personality test that conforms perfectly to this twenty-first century workplace. The (MBTI's) unfailingly positive tone blends seamlessly with the language of corporate political correctness and with our society's emphasis on promoting self-esteem. The euphemistic blandness of the Myers-Briggs, its mild vocabulary of "fit" and "gift", is the key to its success . . .'[4]

Paul argued that the idea that an individual's personality should 'fit' a particular job is an attempt to shift responsibility from performance to a lack of harmony between employee and organisation. Neither individuals nor organisations are good or bad. When things go wrong, it is a lack of 'fit' that is the culprit. It is a conveniently fatalistic philosophy. Since workers can't grow into new responsibilities and managers can't be expected to accommodate their developing abilities, personality functions as an escape valve, letting off pressures for personal freedom and organisational change and distracts managers from such questions as whether work is fairly managed and adequately paid.

After World War II the personality testing business boomed. Cattell's *16 Personality Factor Questionnaire* and many other personality tests competed for managers' purses. But then for some quaint reason the number 'five' became fashionable. American personologists rushed into print claiming that the 18,000 traits found in a good dictionary can be reduced to five – the *Big Five* – extraversion, agreeableness, conscientiousness, emotional stability (not included in the MBTI), and openness to experience.

In 1968 Walter Mischel published *Personality and Assessment* which had a devastating effect on the collective conscience of personologists. Mischel outlined several confusions in their field. First, 'personality' and 'behaviour' are often used interchangeably. Whereas behaviour consists of observable events, personality is an abstraction inferred from behaviour. Second, 'trait' is used in a variety of ways: to refer to the differences between the observed behaviour of two or more individuals, and as a personality construct invented for its explanatory power but which does not have any concrete existence as a 'thing' or 'process' within a person. However, many personologists (such as Cattell) have treated traits as if they are processes that *exist in* persons. Third, traits have been treated as *causes* of behaviour when it is clear that abstractions cannot have causal power. Fourth, some personologists treat traits as if they are 'mental structures' which are pervasive and enduring. Fifth, it is often asserted that because individuals respond differently to environmental stimuli, personality traits must be invoked as the explanation. Sixth, some personologists believe personality traits are inherited, although it is hard to imagine that, say, conscientiousness is inherited. Seventh, it is often claimed that personality traits can be measured and predict individual behaviour although research studies consistently invalidate this claim.

Mischel argued that the massive attention to personality traits has been accompanied by an equally massive neglect of environmental factors. Unless the environment changes significantly, past behaviour rather than personality test scores remains the best predictor of future behaviour in similar situations. Personology leads one to infer enduring generalised attributes in persons and to predict from the inferred trait to behaviour in various situations. This would be an appropriate procedure if it could be done reliably and provided predictive power. But, Mischel argued, more than five decades of research have shown conclusively that it cannot. He concluded that traits are excessively crude concepts to encompass adequately the subtlety of human behaviour.

The years following the publication of Mischel's book are universally described as 'dark' ones for the field of personality testing. According to Paul, personology experienced a major crisis, it was 'mired in Mischellian mud'. But it didn't take long to exchange one mud bath for another. After acknowledging the influence of social conditioning, which they had never denied, personologists sallied forth under the banner of *interactionism*. Unfortunately, the environmentalists of the 1960s were losing ground to the biological reductionists of the 1980s, and when the Big Five taxonomy was revived Mischel's work was consigned to history.

Mischel acknowledged that trait measures provide useful summaries of average differences among individuals and groups, but he questioned the psychological meaning of the traits that are inferred from these measures. Furthermore, the trait approach provides relatively little in the way of psychological theory and explanation. It is insufficient (and circular) to say that she is friendly because she is an extravert. Mischel noted how the revival of the Big Five model generated fresh enthusiasm for the trait model but pointed to its considerable limitations.

During the 1990s there were several meta-analyses which investigated the relationship between the five magic bullets and work performance. Meta-analysis, which became very popular in the 1980s, combines the published findings of several studies in a similar field and weights then insofar as it is possible on the basis of relevant data. Inevitably, researchers disagree about many aspects of this procedure and there is much room for 'creative' interpretation. One rule is clear (or should be): meta-analytical researchers of the Big Five should not include in their data studies that use measures other than those that measure the Big Five. But this is exactly what they did. And so the results of the rival reviews differed quite significantly, spawning a public controversy as authors challenged each other's professional competence. While later meta-analyses have addressed these basic methodological issues, the findings are meagre.

I have managed to get this far in the discussion without burdening the reader with statistics. But it is now necessary to mention one – the correlation coefficient – which measures the relationship between two variables. If we want to measure how much information about the value of Y can be obtained from a knowledge of the corresponding value of X, we measure the degree of correlation between X and Y When there is some degree of correlation between X and Y, then information about an X value contains some information about the corresponding Y value. The value of the correlation coefficient ranges from –1 through 0 to +1. When an individual has the same rank on X and Y, the correlation is perfect and has a value of +1. When a correlation is positive but less than perfect, low scores on X are associated imperfectly with low scores on Y. When X and Y are unrelated, the correlation coefficient is 0.

In connection with any quantity which varies, such as job performance, a question can be asked about sources of variation. Does the variation arise solely because of differences among personalities? Certainly not. So the correlation coefficient can be used as an indicator of the proportion of the variation in job performance which is related to personality scores. The correlation thus provides an answer to the question: how much does the variation in personality contribute to the variation which occurs in job performance? This question may be answered in terms of *variance*. The square of the correlation coefficient indicates the proportion of variation in job performance which is *accounted for* by differences in personality scores. If the correlation between job performance and personality scores is +.9 (which it has never been) then the proportion of variance accounted for is 81 per cent (and 19 per cent is unaccounted for) and personality would be a very strong predictor of job performance. For 50 per cent of the variance of job performance to be accounted for by personality a correlation coefficient of just over +.7 is required. Since important employment decisions are based on the assumption that personality scores predict job performance, one would expect and hope that the correlation coefficients are greater than +.7 otherwise decision makers will make a large number of *rejecting* and *accepting* errors.

What have the meta-analyses found? Four meta-analytic studies of the relationship between job performance and personality scores yielded the following average correlation coefficients: conscientiousness .21; neuroticism .15; extraversion .13; agreeableness .13; openness to experience .12. These results are worrying enough since the much-quoted result of .21 for conscientiousness means that the proportion of variance unaccounted for is 95.6 per cent. Responsible decisions about hiring, promotion or training cannot be made on the basis of these figures.

However, the actual situation is far worse since it makes an important difference to the results when personality scores are correlated with 'hard' or 'soft' performance criteria. Soft criteria include subjective ratings whereas hard criteria include productivity data, salary, turnover/tenure, change of status. Since personality scores are better predictors of subjective performance ratings than objective performance measures, it is reasonable to conclude that raters rely on personality when evaluating job performance, thereby raising the question whether the relationship between personality and performance is the result of the bias of the rater rather than actual performance. In the much-quoted study by Barrick and Mount the correlation coefficient dropped from .26 for soft criteria to .14 for hard criteria. The average correlation between the Big Five and job performance (hard criteria) was .07.[5]

It has been a standing joke for more than fifty years that personality testing is known as the '.2 industry' meaning that the proportion of variance accounted for between personality and job performance is at best, 4 per cent. It is surely a scandal that important decisions about individuals' careers are based on such a cavalier disregard for empirical results.

After rehearsing these arguments for forty years I have become aware (as a slow learner) that neither invalid logic nor lack of scientific evidence bothers testers. Nor do the findings, suitably researched and published in respectable journals, that personality tests are discriminatory, unreliable, invalid, easily faked, and cannot predict management performance though they are used for that purpose. Since personality test scores are unrelated to management performance, there is no way to determine 'fit' with the corporate culture, and so 'fit' must be determined by other, often unstated criteria, such as getting on with the boss. Sadly, in our postmodern, politically correct, new age world of business, disagreeing with the boss, or indeed anyone, is likely to get one into trouble. People who argue with their managers are likely to be accused of low 'emotional intelligence' and subjected to psychometric tests, counselling, coaching and further invasions of their privacy.

One American who was not prepared to tolerate such an invasion of privacy took the matter to court.[6] An aspiring Californian actor, Sibi Soroka, applied for a job as a security guard with Target Stores, a discount retailer owned by Dayton Hudson Corporation. All job applicants for security officer positions were required to undertake a psychological test – Psychscreen – which is a version of the Minnesota Multiphasic Personality Inventory (MMPI) and the California Psychological Inventory (CPI). The MMPI was designed to identify 'deviant personalities' and the CPI to assess 'emotional responsibility'. Both of these tests have been routinely used to screen out emotionally unfit applicants for such positions as police officers, pilots, air traffic controllers and nuclear power plant operators. Psychscreen eliminates the overlap between the tests and takes about four hours to complete. Target began using it in 1988 to identify and reject applicants who were supposedly emotionally unstable. Test results are evaluated by a firm of psychologists – Martin-McAllister – who provide Target with applicants' numerical ratings and a general recommendation as to whether the person poses a security risk. Karen Grabow, a Target executive, said that she would not expect to see the calibre of the whole workforce improve as a result of this test but would expect that Psychscreen might identify 'lunatics' and keep them out of her organisation.

Psychscreen consists of 704 true/false statements and includes questions of a religious nature, such as:

67. I feel sure that there is only one true religion . . .
477. My soul sometimes leaves my body . . .
506. I believe in the second coming of Christ . . .

688. I believe there is a Devil and a Hell in afterlife.

Psychscreen also includes items of a frankly sexual nature, such as:

290. I have never been in trouble because of my sex behaviour . . .

492. I am very strongly attracted by members of my own sex . . .

496. I have often wished I were a girl. (Or if you are a girl) I have never been sorry that I am a girl . . .

525. I have never indulged in any unusual sex practices . . .

Psychologists rate the applicants on six traits: emotional stability, response set, interpersonal style, addiction potential, dependability and reliability, and socialisation.

Sibi Soroka, Susan Urry and William d'Arcangelo were applicants for security officer positions when they took the test. All three were upset by the nature of the test questions. Soroka was hired whereas Urry (a Mormon) and d'Arcangelo were not. In August 1989 Soroka filed a charge with the Department of Fair Employment and Housing that use of Psychscreen discriminated on the basis of race, sex and religion. In September class action was filed against Target to prohibit its use of Psychscreen. A professional psychologist submitted a declaration arguing that the use of the test was unjustified and improper and that its use violated professional standards since it had not been shown to be reliable or valid as an employment tool. Soroka added that two of Target's experts had previously said that the MMPI was virtually useless as a pre-employment device. It was also reported that Psychscreen resulted in a 61 per cent rate of false positives, i.e. more than six in ten qualified applicants were not hired. Target submitted declarations contesting these accusations and favouring continued use of the test as an employment screening tool. Soroka's lawyer argued, and Target conceded, that Psychscreen

revealed personal information. But under California's consti-
tution an individual's right to privacy can be overridden by a
stronger social interest. The core of the case, therefore, turned on
the question of whether Target's interest in ensuring an emotionally stable workforce justified the invasion of privacy caused by
the use of Psychscreen. Lawyers for Soroka argued that religious
and sex items are discriminatory because they are not related
to work performance. Target's lawyers argued that these items
could identify emotionally unstable individuals. (Question: Are
people who believe in the devil emotionally unstable given the
fact that the majority of Americans believe in the devil? How
would Psychscreen be scored in Australia where very few people
believe in the devil?)

On October 25, 1991 a California court of appeals ruled in
favour of allowing Soroka to proceed to trial. The court found
that Target had failed to demonstrate a compelling interest or
a job-related purpose connected with Psychscreen's religious
and sex items. Target appealed and in January 1992 the California Supreme Court agreed to hear the case. But while Soroka
waited, new legislation took effect which impacted on his case.
The *Americans with Disabilities Act* of 1990 (ADA) prohibited
job discrimination against a qualified individual because of a
disability. The ADA required that pre-employment physical or
medical examinations be related to the relevant job. In Soroka's
case the question was obvious: would the ADA apply to a personality test? Soroka believed it would since it would be perceived
as a medical examination. If so, the court could find that the use
of a personality test violated the ADA.

In the summer of 1993 Target executives agreed to settle
without admitting liability and agreed to exempt Californian
job applicants from Psychscreen. On advice Target placed
$1.3 million in a fund to be divided among those who had taken
Psychscreen. Soroka and the other two plaintiffs were awarded

$60,000 and Soroka settled for $22,000. Soroka concluded that he wanted to be evaluated on his record of performance, not on what he does on Sunday or in the bedroom.

Australian managers might also pay attention to a 2009 American case – *Wilson versus Johnson & Johnson* – in which the plaintiff sued his former employer for irreparable damages that resulted from the over-use of personality tests. The jurors agreed that excessive testing caused psychological strain and led to unnecessary scrutiny resulting in personal grief. Wilson was awarded $US4.7 million.

It is a lamentable fact that personologists claim to know about personality but cannot agree among themselves on fundamental issues. At least 200 competing definitions are available to the perplexed student of personality, most of them so vague as to be worthless. The only theme which can be extracted from the less ambiguous definitions is that personality is known through the observation of relatively *consistent tendencies* in people's behaviour. These are referred to internal traits which are conceived of as exerting control over their conduct and thereby constituting an explanation of it.

First, consistency of behaviour over situations is not a sufficient condition for the inference of personality traits because the consistent behaviour associated with role-playing and habits are acquired skills which help people achieve their goals. Second, where people are ignorant of potentially effective behaviour (say, in another culture) their ineffective behaviour cannot be attributed to personality traits. Third, the conditions under which personality traits may be inferred are therefore: a person's behaviour must be consistent over situations in which it is effective; when behaviour is ineffective it must not be the result of a person's ignorance since they should have had the opportunity to adapt their behaviour to the circumstances. It follows from these three points that the only behaviour which may be attributed to personality traits is that which implies a *lack of adaptability*. This is consistent with the allegedly stable character of personality traits. Since adaptability and the capacity to acquire skills are closely related to or even identical with intelligence, personality is by definition *negatively related to intelligence*. In other words, personality traits are whatever reduces the flexibility of individuals' behaviour and makes them unable to act intelligently.

What then are we to make of emotional intelligence? If the advocates of emotional intelligence believe that one should express one's emotions intelligently it is difficult to disagree with them. It is, however, easy to disagree with the assumption that underpins this popular topic: emotional intelligence is a *personality trait*. If so, it is negatively related to (cognitive) intelligence: it is *unintelligent intelligence*.

6

Unintelligent Intelligence

Intelligence tests: Politically correct way of dividing them from us; bag of tricks invented by psychologists and used by managers to assess entry into their profession, but excludes nobody.

A newly minted manager received the following letter:

Dear Colleague,

Congratulations. You have been selected from a large number of candidates to attend our Advanced Management Conference to be held at the Easyrest Resort.

Your management have, with the help of highly qualified consultants, designed this year's conference to maximise your management potential so that, going forward, you can progress. Our consultants will talk to you about motivation, communication, team-building and emotional intelligence and there will be many opportunities for you to share your feelings with each other. We in senior management believe that it is important to develop a well-rounded personality and strong team spirit so that all may blend into our corporate culture. We value understanding each other, helping each other in difficult times and working together as a happy and motivated team. We believe in a management style that is people-oriented so that a collective need for achievement may emerge.

Your performance at the conference will not be rated. We are vitally interested in your *potential*. Our consultants will help us identify those of you who have potential to progress in the company. We trust that this search for executive potential will not place you under stress. Please remember to be yourself and you will get the most from this experience, going forward. My colleagues in senior management congratulate you on your selection and wish you well during your challenging course.

Yours affectionately,
Director of Human Resources, Leadership and Learning.

The recipient of this letter was an engineer in his late 30s who had been told that his career path would take him out of engineering and into management. Accordingly, he was 'invited' to the five-day management course announced in the letter. Like a lamb to the slaughter he delivered himself into the hands of three 'facilitators', ('lecturer' is an authoritarian term in the postmodern world), who told the reluctant participants to stop thinking logically (like engineers) and express their feelings. The purpose of the course was to enable the engineers and accountants to get in touch with their feelings and thereby increase their emotional intelligence. Whenever the engineer attempted to debate with the facilitators, he was forcibly reminded that his behaviour betrayed emotional insensitivity. When he asked what emotional intelligence had to do with management he was told: everything!

The concept of intelligence has had a wonderfully contro-versial history in psychology. It started with French government bureaucrats believing that some children were too dull to benefit from their fine schools. They decided that a short test was needed to separate those having the ability to glorify the schools from the unfortunates who did not. The test was invented by one of France's most respected psychologists, Alfred Binet, who invented tests of cognitive abilities and formed them into a scale for schoolchildren. Since cognitive ability increases with age, norms were obtained for different ages and individuals' scores related to the distribution for their age. Later, psychologists divided the 'mental age' by the chronological age to obtain a ratio called the 'intelligence quotient' or IQ. The Binet test was revised at Stanford University (in 1916) and this version was adopted by American psychologists for at least twenty years thereafter. Testing was also used during the First World War to exclude the retarded from the US military forces.

Psychologists were quick to see that this type of test had the potential for practical applications and, accordingly, intelligence test-making became a dominating preoccupation of psycho-logists. The construction of these tests depended on the use of statistical techniques of correlation. The aim was to select a number of different problems for their power to tap a similar type of ability and then graduate them according to difficulty. Items which failed to meet these criteria were discarded since they did not tap the same kind of ability. And so separate tests, such as numeracy, vocabulary and pattern perception, were produced, the scores added and the total converted by stand-ardising against age norms.

To the surprise of psychologists it was found that the scales which had been purified so as to be scales of separate abilit-ies always correlated positively with one another. While the correlations were not high, they were never negative. This led

English psychologist Charles Spearman to invent a mathematical method of extracting what was common to groups of tests. Factor analysis produced a large common factor, which he called g (for general intelligence) and a smaller specific factor for each test. Spearman used the result to propound a two-factor theory of intelligence, each performance being held to consist of an element of general intelligence and a task-specific element. In Chicago, L Thurstone promoted five factors that were more involved than others in successful cognitive performances and named them 'primary mental abilities'.

The disagreement between Spearman and Thurstone generated a heated debate. The Americans were offended by Spearman's theory. It was suggested that the different results arose from cultural biases, in that English society was constructed on a framework of class divisions, so that the English regarded generalists as having the higher class of intellect. Americans, on the other hand, regarded their society as more democratic and promoted a theory which did not elevate one type of intellect above all others. What seems more likely is that the difference arose from the difficulty of arriving at a rapprochement between mathematical and verbal skills.

American psychologists have consistently promoted a multi-factor definition of intelligence as can be seen in the popular book by Stephen Jay Gould, *The Mismeasure of Man*. In the 1990s an American psychologist toured Australia arguing for seven separate intelligences. His rationale was that if teachers are encouraged to view the notion of intelligence in this way they will be less likely to downgrade students who show weakness in one area, but will try to locate their possible strengths in other areas.

In the early decades of the twentieth century Cyril Burt argued that inheritance was a strong influence in intelligence, but this idea has never been popular in the US and long after

Burt's death American psychologists claimed that he had fudged his data to favour his theory. While the circumstantial evidence supports this accusation, falsifying one set of scientific results is not sufficient to invalidate the theory that heredity is a factor. Numerous other studies, including some very extensive American work, suggest that it is important. But how important heredity is cannot be stated categorically. The usual ambit of positive claims is around 60 per cent to heredity against 40 per cent to environment. As heredity and environment interact, intelligent parents often have intelligent children but almost always the children of intelligent parents get the best environment to grow in. So also do parents lacking in intelligence tend to have children with similar failings but also tend to provide a less adequate educational environment.

Teachers are employed to teach, of course. Teaching is often hard work, so to keep up their own spirits and fortify themselves against the ravages of despair they are inclined to trumpet the doctrine of environmental predominance. They have to do so in order to support the basic rationale of their profession. But it is still the case, after a century of striving among educationalists and psychologists, and many optimistic claims for remedial regimes, that it has been found impossible to educate some sections of the child population beyond certain limits. (Today many teachers attribute this failure to ADHD which is treated with Ritalin – amphetamine with a PG rating).

The debate about intelligence testing became even more acrimonious when numerous research reports purported to show that the average IQ among black Americans was lower than that among white Americans. Among those who accepted these measurements as valid, this has been seen as (a) providing a reason why whites and blacks should be treated differently, or (b) providing a justification for the existing differences in treatment. Of course the fact of a difference in IQ (if fact there is) carries *no* such implications at all. It is the same kind of statement as an engineer might make in comparing the relative strengths of two metals. Questions of different treatments arise only when they are considered as factors involved in something we want to achieve. But it is easy to take up the false implication; so easy that the case of the black Americans' IQ has aroused great passion. One reaction has been to impugn the validity of IQ tests. Properly constructed tests, it has been claimed, would show the black Americans to be the intellectual equal of white Americans and therefore entitled to equal treatment. This last implication is just as invalid as the original. Whether people are equal or not has no logical connection with whether they should be treated as equal. The latter is a moral choice and if it were logically tied to the actual status of equality we would be hard put to find any two people entitled to equal treatment.

Of the same family of errors is a tendency found among some feminists who point out that females (on average) are equal in IQ to males. Therefore, they argue, they are entitled to the same range of positions in the economic system as males. There is, of course, no logical connection. We may take it as a fact that the average IQ among females does not differ from that among males. Yet this does not bind us to any choice, moral or other, as to how they should spend their lives. Only if we hold to some principle that all people of equal IQ should be of equal rank in the economic system does the fact of equal IQs become pertinent.

These examples contain an element of farce, so we are inclined to say that those who make such errors are merely individuals whose discussion shows little academic merit. Surely, we think, such superficial problems cannot spell decay and death for psychology. But they are in fact very threatening, for such crusades foster the belief that what we are concerned with is reforming society by making choices which eliminate moral problems as they arise. People have been doing this for centuries with methods like preaching, propaganda, legal enforcement, appeals to emotion, bullying, even war, all of which pre-date scientific psychology and all of which can successfully change things as intended. But they do more. Changes reverberate through society and result in a whole complex of unintended effects, so that society becomes a different system, which suffers from new problems.

A case in point is the widespread belief that intelligence tests are incomplete measures of the 'total personality' because they ignore emotional skills, even though most personality tests measure emotionality/anxiety/neuroticism. In the 1990s it was fashionable to suggest that cognitive intelligence is only half as important as 'emotional intelligence'. This gave rise to numerous tests of 'emotional intelligence' and the problems of reliability and validity arose again.

It has to be admitted that the reliability and validity of the measurement of intelligence hoped for by psychologists has proved elusive, but not so elusive that measurement is useless. One thing that disagreement about the measurement of this abstract property has stimulated is a good deal of thinking about the nature of intelligence.

'Intelligence' is an abstract noun which describes a particular *relationship*. One acts intelligently; one does not *have* intelligence. Intelligence, therefore, is an ability (or collection of abilities) which manifests itself in interactions between individuals and their environment. Unlike other species of animals, human beings can not only survive in almost any natural environment but invent novel ways of coping if the environment changes. The facts of evolution tell us that this extreme spread of capabilities must be seen as the distinguishing feature of human intelligence. Central to it is the quality of *versatility*.

If versatility is at the heart of intelligence it is unlikely that it can be measured with the kind of precision required by the canons of science, or that we would ever need to. IQ tests were always intended to be short samples of problem-solving ability that would give a useful indication of those likely to fail, or be very slow, at learning the kinds of skills required in Western-style education. They do this quite well and it is surely unnecessary to demand that they should measure some highly abstract concept like intelligence.

Children necessarily approach the matter from a totally different point of view from that of adults. From an early age they learn to do many things which require them to be skilled performers and each new achievement augments their identity as active agents in the world. In almost all these learning tasks they are required to do no more than follow the pattern offered by their parents, guardians, companions and they learn directly from them. When they enter formal schooling they find the business of learning new skills complicated by a constant process of evaluation of each performance, in which teachers act as the imposer of public standards. This new condition hugely empha-sises the importance of performing effectively, and it does so over a wide range of skills and through long periods of training, so that it is borne in upon students that their own personal powers – as demonstrated by their performance record – and also the personal powers of others are of supreme importance. This eventually becomes an assumption implicit in their world view. Thus the concept of 'self' which emerges around the age of three years goes on developing as the original potentialities of individuals unfold through interaction with the kinds of reality they encounter in their progress towards autonomy. They are (theoretically) held by their training to a straight-line develop-ment towards becoming self-managing individuals with a sound knowledge of their own powers.

Through the education process learners are repeatedly confronted by the standards offered by teachers. A large proportion of these are based on simple logic, as in elementary mathematics, and if learners dispute these they are likely to be called mentally incompetent. This statement has to be qualified in the light of the fact that postmodernists, if they are sincere in their beliefs, are disinclined to accept the validity of logical demonstrations, although they (insincerely) accept the rules of arithmetic. Many other customarily accepted standards are by no means clear-cut and some shade off into realms of the vague and disputable, so that they frequently need to be supported and maintained by sanctions of an arbitrary character. Standards of the latter kind, which mainly apply to things like the way individuals conduct themselves towards others, introduce learners to the notion of authority as something which defines what is right and wrong in the exercise of power by both individuals and groups. At the same time the sanctions which support them are recognised as exercises of social power independent of individuals.

After only a few years of regular education students' perspectives of the social world begin to take shape. In this phenomenal world individuals are the centre, and they are defined by their repertoire of tried and tested abilities and (on a vaguer level) by the things they think might be within their powers. They see themselves as embedded in an overwhelmingly powerful society which claims the authority to say what they may and may not do, and have the power to punish them if they break the rules. There is an obvious possibility of conflict between the doctrine which encourages them to develop all their potentialities to become autonomous and the authority code which forbids them to do certain things. Realisation of this, particularly if it is occasioned by actual collision with authority and the experience of punishment, often generates a tendency to rebellion and hostility towards the wielders of power. Many young people go through such a phase in their development, and it is frequently succeeded by another phase in which rebellion by individuals is replaced by group agreement on one particular style of rebellion, which in turn leads the rebels into their own style of conformity. Through conformity of course they can, and often do, discover that society does not use its power solely to administer punishment, but can also dispense rewards. Authority is by far the most effective protector of the weak against the rule of force.

Lessons such as these were taught in Victorian times through the study of the 'Classics': the commentators on social history that we have inherited from ancient Greece and Rome. But schooling is subject to fashions, and these are often dictated by politics, by religions, by ideologies, or simply by popular enthusiasms. The present fashion is to teach 'cultural studies' which is claimed to be more to the point than the comments of Roman senators, poets and the journalists of ancient times. While I doubt this, I don't think it really matters. Recognition of the part played by power in the structure of society is virtually inescapable, because if we did not need to generate power beyond what is possible for individuals acting solo, we would not need to organise groups at all. If we could organise to generate such power without requiring that individuals obey rules that over-ride their personal predilections we would not need an authority code.

It would be impossible to prevent anyone who undergoes a normal education from arriving at the cognitive map of society I have described, in which power is primary and authority its necessary moderator, unless people suffered from a freakish inability to abstract from empirical events.

In the course of schooling students steadily develop in intelligence by learning the meanings of scores of other abstract names for relationships – hate, love, enmity, desire, dominance, submission, friendship, romance, competition, cooperation – and their meaning will be distinguished by the actions which are observed to identify them and the feelings which accompany them. Some of these play very important parts in workplace relationships. It comes as no surprise, therefore, to read books whose authors state the obvious: to become mature individuals we need to be knowledgeable of and versatile with respect to our emotions – we need emotional skills. If intelligence (in any form) is synonymous with versatility, we will make a grave error to treat emotional intelligence as a personality trait. But that is exactly what the emotional intelligence movement does.

The history of the emotional intelligence movement is easily summarised, even if there is little agreement within the movement about definitions, measures and outcomes. This is a familiar story to anyone who has flirted with personologists or consulted the personality trait literature.

Emotional intelligence, or the ability to emote effectively, is as old as Western philosophy. The Stoics, for example, believed that one should live one's life rationally in agreement with nature. While individuals are restricted by nature and society in many ways, they are nonetheless free to choose their emotions. They believed that rational individuals will choose to free themselves from worldly demands, negative emotions and excessive pleasure-seeking. Of three possible life-styles – the contemplative, the practical and the rational – the Stoics argued for the latter because, while human beings have been created for contemplation and action, the universe is governed by reason and fate and individuals of 'character' exercise their reason and calmly accept their fate. Individuals of character do not allow themselves to fall victim to such self-defeating emotions as hostility, depression or anxiety. One should live in accordance with the plan of reality which can be comprehended by reason and make one's desires identical with that plan. Fools try to impose their own ideas upon reality and come to grief. Unhappiness is the result of allowing one's egoism to flout the dictates of reason and reality. One should not wish for desires: one should desire what one gets. These ideas had considerable impact on the Roman Empire through the works of Epictetus and Marcus Aurelius. Epictetus, for example, argued that people upset themselves not by things but by their view of them. He invited his readers to inspect their powers of reason for in these lie their abilities to control their passions. He did not suggest that one should be passionless, like a statue. Rather, he encouraged people to cultivate self-promoting emotions which help them maintain satisfactory social relations.

After reading the Stoics it is difficult to understand why emotional intelligence was considered either new or interesting, until one realises that the ancient philosophers' emphasis on rationality and freewill was unacceptable to personologists who were committed to the deterministic view that emotions are not chosen but are part of one's personality structure. This is frankly acknowledged by the promoters of emotional intelligence who claimed that the only assumption that the numerous and contradictory definitions of emotional intelligence share is that EI is a *personality trait*.

It was the faddish decade of the 1990s that ushered in the craze for emotional intelligence tests. An editorial in the journal *Intelligence* in 1993 argued for the existence of an emotional intelligence trait, science journalist Daniel Goleman wrote a best-seller, *Emotional Intelligence*, with the instructive sub-title, *Why it can matter more than IQ*, and *Time* Magazine had a cover featuring 'EQ'. By 1997 there were several EQ scales and, inevitably, vigorous debate about their reliability and validity.

The fashion in management circles of speaking of one's ability to recognise the meanings of emotions and feelings as 'intelligence' can be viewed as either a trivial re-definition of cognitive intelligence, or yet another attempt by psychologists to impose a personological perspective on the community by asserting that emotional intelligence is a personality trait. That it is the latter perspective which has excited psychologists and seduced a gullible public is illustrated and supported by the number of 'emotional intelligence' (EQ) tests competing for managers' purses. A popular view is that EQ includes everything related to success (variously defined) that is not measured by IQ. Now while IQ does indeed predict job performance to a modest degree, there is no evidence that EQ (whatever it means) does so. This suggests that, unlike IQ which is a measure of abilities, conceptualising and measuring EQ as a personality trait, condemns it to suffer the same fate as the other personality traits. And like personality traits, there is no general agreement among psychologists about their meaning: extraversion means 'sociability' for some (American) psychologists and 'changeability' for some (English) psychologists. Cognitive intelligence has been reasonably defined; emotional intelligence has not. Definitions range from specific cognitive abilities to amorphous models that include personality and motivational traits, and there is considerable overlap in the measurement of cognitive and emotional intelligence. It is difficult to resist the conclusion that the popularity of emotional intelligence is faddish and little more than low-grade personality research. This is surely a disappointing conclusion after more than twenty years of attempts by psychologists to define and measure the construct. In short, the field is a mess and mass of propaganda.

By the 1990s emotional intelligence was firmly entrenched in management training courses and seriously promoted by human resource managers, especially females. If females saw emotional intelligence as an ability that they possessed to a greater degree than males, it is understandable that they would promote it. And promote it they did.

It is clear that emotional intelligence in the twenty-first century is not intended to mean what it meant to the ancient

Greeks. Rather, the proponents of emotional intelligence inverted the views of the ancients by promoting the expression of feelings as a substitute for, or inversion of, rational thinking. And since some feminists associate rational thinking with some of the worst excesses of masculinity, it is easy to understand why emotional intelligence would appeal to them. As more females enter the ranks of management and seek competitive advantage, some will seek to invert the fundamental assumptions of the (male-dominated) Western rational tradition which extols rational, critical thinking and indicts the expression of feelings. A feminist inversion of values, therefore, would involve the idea that expressing feelings should be valued and encouraged. Those individuals who retire behind the façade of rational thinking can be considered 'emotionally suppressed'. High EQ can then be interpreted as a positive virtue. Managers, especially males, who do not value the expression of personal feelings will need to be trained to overcome their inhibitions. In proportion as expressing one's feelings is encouraged, arguing with one's colleagues is discouraged. There is a logical reason for this. Propositions which express feelings are neither true nor false, whereas propositions which describe a state of affairs must be either true or false. Arguments are either valid or invalid, and feelings are, well, feelings.

There is an important relationship between the various functions of language and personal values. For example, managers who emphasise 'commanding' language betray a value system which differs from those who emphasise 'suggesting' language, which is why they are called the Ten Commandments and not the Ten Suggestions. Similarly, managers who argue value clarity of thinking because they realise that descriptive propositions are often ambiguous: metaphors abound and one has to make due allowance for them. When we say that a person's mind has gone blank we recognise the metaphor. But when we state that a person's mind is ill, we are less likely to do so. When it is claimed that managers are scientists, artists, politicians, coaches, captains or leaders, we are clearly in the grip of metaphor. As if this isn't enough, the management literature is replete with oxymorons (two words which yield a self-contradiction, e.g. military intelligence, entrepreneurial management, fun run); pleonasms (two words which yield a redundancy, e.g. strategic management, reverting back, freezing cold); and tautologies (expanded pleonasms, e.g. leaders influence people, charismatics have special personal qualities, managers are paid professionals).

Lynda Spillane found that managers in the Australian public service did not like to argue with their colleagues, preferring to employ the language of technical authority.[1] Her findings are consistent with local research which shows that managers favour a collaborative style of communication which shuns argument because of the fear that it might generate conflict. The desire to avoid overt conflict in work relationships, and the inability to cope with it when it arises, is a recurring theme in studies of Australian managers who describe the essential elements of the management relationship as trust, honesty, fairness and respect. The majority of the managers in her study acknowledged that they rarely argued with their colleagues because it involves excessive emotion and is rarely, if ever, constructive. Arguing, they thought, was a last resort when questioning failed. Managers saw arguing as stating one's point of view and putting forward negative sentiments for the opposite view, which is a pointless waste of time. Arguing was also seen as an invitation to engage in aggressive behaviour which reduces their authority. Thus, the widespread use of 'it seems to me', 'in my opinion' and 'subjectively speaking' as defences against criticism. This view of argument is far removed from the ancients Greeks who valued argument as the sign of intellectual maturity.

To argue is to give *reasons* to support one's description of a state of affairs. And this is why the Western intellectual tradition, which has for more than 2500 years based itself squarely on argument as the vehicle for personal and social development, is called the Western *rational* tradition. Or at least it was until the arrival of postmodernists.

Since the rise of postmodernism in the 1970s arguing has been seen as unduly masculine, aggressive and ill-mannered behaviour. In 1981 American philosopher Robert Nozick argued that the savage practice of arguing is coercive because if, in a valid deductive argument, you accept the premises you *have* to accept the conclusion. Argument is, for Nozick, an attempt to force people to accept conclusions they don't *feel good* about. He asked plaintively: 'Why are philosophers intent on forcing others to believe things? Is that a nice way to behave toward someone?' He answered his own question: 'No, that is not a nice way to behave toward someone.'[2]

What, then, are we to make of the role of emotional intelligence in management? It has been said that IQ gets one hired and EQ gets one promoted. Such assertions are based on claims, by Daniel Goleman for example, that emotional intelligence predicts success in producing effective teamwork. However, he is unable to cite published empirical evidence to support his assertion. While there are many anecdotal, impressionistic and self-serving accounts, there are *no* empirical studies which show that emotional intelligence predicts management performance. Most of the popular claims about the relationship between emotional intelligence and work success are misleading and pretentious. They are misleading because they pretend to be offering empirical evidence, when they are in fact relying on impression and propaganda.

Once the idea of multiple intelligences is accepted there is no limit to the number of specific types which can be defined, discussed and measured – cognitive, emotional, social, political, organisational, leadership, business, money-making, criminal, alcoholic, musical, moral, spiritual, and so on. The old theory of multiple intelligences has never been more popular and there are many books, popular and academic, extolling the virtues of many types of intelligence. Indeed, one is drawn to the conclusion that there are as many types of human intelligence as there are types of human ability. Is the ability to make a cup of coffee an example of (coffee-making) intelligence? We have a right to wonder why authors insist on referring to specific abilities as intelligences, especially when many abilities are not correlated with measures of cognitive intelligence.

One of the appealing aspects of the theory of multiple intelligences is that it allows all people to be intelligent in their own way and thus maintain self-esteem. One may be deficient in mathematical intelligence, but espousing particular values – spiritual intelligence – can serve as a self-enhancing substitute.

In 2002 Danah Zohar and Ian Marshall advertised a series of workshops at Macquarie University based on Spiritual Intelligence (SQ), a concept that they argued is firmly grounded in quantum physics and recent research in the field of neurophysiology. As quantum physics is a system of *mechanics* used to explain the behaviour of atoms, molecules and elementary particles, it is difficult to see how it could provide support for spiritual intelligence, whatever that term means. The authors claimed that unlike IQ which is applicable to computers, and EQ which exists in higher mammals, SQ is unique to human beings. It is, they claimed, linked to our need for meaning and is what we use to develop our capacity for vision, values, and purpose. Apparently, we use SQ to be flexible, visionary and creatively spontaneous and it enables us to inspire others and be inspired ourselves. Furthermore, it represents the 'power of inner leadership' which is truly miraculous given that 'leadership' is a relationship between leader and followers. Presumably, 'inner' leadership means that one part of us (the spiritual) leads and the other (the non-spiritual?) follows. The workshops were over-subscribed and the audience rated them highly.

Once they leave the field of spiritual intelligence managers are confronted by books on 'moral' intelligence. An example is a 2005 book, *Moral Intelligence*, by Lennick and Kiel with an enthusiastic recommendation from Daniel Goleman. The book includes a 'measure' of moral intelligence – the Moral Competency Inventory (MCI) – which includes the following statements:

- I tell the truth unless there is an overriding reason to withhold it.
- I own up to my own mistakes and failures.
- My leadership approach is to lead by serving others.
- When I forgive someone, I find that it benefits me as much as it does them.
- My co-workers would say that I am a compassionate person.
- When someone asks me to keep a confidence, I do so.

Morally intelligent individuals allegedly value integrity, responsibility, compassion and forgiveness. The authors make two claims. First, they believe that these values are to be praised and promoted. Second, they claim that managers need to espouse these values if they are to prosper. They assert that 'there is a powerful correlation between strong moral principles and business success' which may be true, and the moral principles which guarantee success are integrity, responsibility, compassion and forgiveness which is not true. A consequence of Lennick's and Kiel's view is that people with high moral intelligence reject and invert the values espoused by Niccolo Machiavelli and popularised by such television programs as *Yes Minister*. Machiavellians, therefore, have low moral intelligence, if the morals happen to be Christian since they do not support or promote notions of compassion, forgiveness or brotherly love. Lennick and Kiel support the Christian proverb, 'honesty is the best policy', rather than the Machiavellian alternative, 'he who tells the truth gets his head bashed in.' Interestingly, Machiavelli does not appear in Lennick's or Kiel's index.

In the 1960s psychologists finally caught up with the great Florentine who died in 1527 after writing one of the most important books on political rulership ever published – *The Prince*. Psychologists plundered the book and, inevitably, constructed 'Machiavellian scales' which generated hundreds of research papers. Individuals who endorsed Machiavelli's views about the importance of power, audacity, ruthlessness, cunning and deceit were characterised by their emotional detachment; those who were opposed to these values were sentimental and emotionally involved with others. Research showed that scores on Mach scales were unrelated to political affiliation, psychopathology and cognitive intelligence. We can add that they are negatively related to emotional and moral intelligence. People with high Mach scores are aggressive, assertive risk-takers, manipulative, dogmatic, high achievers and masculine. In short, Machiavellians are tough-minded individuals. There is some evidence that they perform better than tender-minded folk in bargaining relationships and are adept at discovering and exploiting personal weaknesses in others. Obviously, Machiavellians lie more and confess less than more sentimental people so that their answers to personality tests cannot be taken at face value. After all, Machiavellians do not admit that they are Machiavellian.

Opinion is still divided about Machiavelli. Clearly he was an anti-Christian writer. But he was also a man of great intelligence who wrote about the realities of politics. If he lacked moral intelligence it is because he understood the political necessity of 'entering into evil when necessity commands'. English philosopher Bertrand Russell wrote: 'It is the custom to be shocked by (Machiavelli), and he certainly is sometimes shocking. But many other men would be equally so if they were equally free from humbug. His political philosophy is scientific and empirical, based upon his own experience of affairs, concerned to set forth the means to assigned ends, regardless of the question whether the ends are to be considered good or bad. When, on occasion, he allows himself to mention the ends that he desires, they are such as we can all applaud. Much of the conventional obloquy that attaches to his name is due to the indignation of hypocrites who hate the frank avowal of evil-doing.'[3]

Machiavelli demonstrated such intellectual honesty about political dishonesty that he was bound to offend moralists who wave their fingers at us because we veer from the path of righteousness. Maurizio Viroli, professor of politics at Princeton University, wrote: '(Machiavelli) knew even too well that human fragility and weakness do not allow for the pursuit of moral perfection, which he also considered to be intolerably boring; he enjoyed the variety of individuals' inclinations, tastes, and passions and never even conceived of the idea that there is but one right way of living one's life. With its misery and its splendour, the human world was the only world that attracted him and for which he cared. His conception of life encompasses different things: the grand and the ordinary, the grave and the light, rigour and transgression, commitment and irony. Many readers will find it confused, unacceptable, or even irritating. I find it a refreshing alternative to the culture of self-interest, reasonableness, and dull decency, as well as the bigotry, the moralism, and the zealotry which pervade our time.'[4]

The moral intelligence movement represents the *tender-minded* alternative to Machiavellianism. By emphasising the importance of integrity, responsibility, compassion and forgiveness – quintessential Christian values – it sets itself against the pagan values of power. If the meek and the mild are to inherit the earth, Christian values of love, compassion and forgiveness must predominate, otherwise the meek and the mild shall be fodder for Machiavelli's ruthless pagans. The moral intelligence movement, therefore, seeks to continue the Christian fight against paganism in management. And their crusaders use the social sciences to help them in their fight.

Certain university subjects suffer from a disadvantage which makes it unlikely – some would say impossible – that they will ever add significantly to human knowledge. Economics, sociology, political science and psychology fall within the category of 'social science'. Each attempts to deal with some aspect of human activity divorced from all other aspects, as if there existed beings who engage only in buying and selling, others who did nothing but knowing, feeling and striving, and so on. This fragmentation of knowledge is largely the result of the ambitions of long-dead scientists and the way they conceived of science. It practically guarantees that these subjects will forever struggle in the shallow soil of pedantic detail.

As if this were not handicap enough, psychology attracts students whose form of egoism inclines them to do good things in the world. These people constitute a considerable temptation to teachers, because it is so easy to achieve popularity among them by portraying one's activities as a means of putting the world to rights. Many teachers fall into the trap of crusading for some popular notion of reform, like equality, or general happiness, or universal mental health. When they do this they have become *moralisers*. They proceed to obscure the all-important distinction between science (as a study of how to do things), and ethics (as as study of man-made rules about what things it is morally desirable to do or not do).

We all do a little harmless moralising from time to time simply because we cannot avoid value judgements when we make decisions. However, there are some who believe that they know, in a very strong sense of the term 'know', precisely how people should act or be prevented from acting, and such is their faith in their own ability to discern how every type of activity will affect the destiny of humanity that they love to infect others with their version of right belief. This is not intelligence, it is *moralism*, and in my experience many psychologists, trainers and authors of management textbooks suffer from it in a most virulent form.

It is a popular belief that science is a means through which the human condition may be improved or ameliorated. Historical cases in which new ways of fighting a disease are discovered illustrate this view. It entirely escapes the attention of moralists (or appears to them to be of no importance) that identifying the cause of a disease empowers us to infect others with it if we wish. Scientific knowledge extends to what we can do, but does not commit us to doing what is morally good with the new power. The naïve faith in science as working for the good of humanity should have been forever destroyed by events originating in nuclear physics. Moralists, however, often react most strangely: holding, for instance, that scientists should refrain from discovering anything which could be used to the disadvantage of humanity. This betokens a total non-comprehension of the nature of scientific activity. Science is directed at discovering how to do things we never previously could do; that is, discovering new forms of power. There cannot be any form of power, new or old, of such a nature that it cannot be used for purposes some would consider immoral.

Suppose that in the near future someone discovers a cure for cancer. Nothing could seem less tainted with immorality. But suppose the discoverer regards his cure as private property, or works for a government who regards it as an official secret; then what is to prevent the owners of the secret from placing any price they please upon access to it? Possession of the secret can readily be used as a means of exploitation, extortion or domination. It can be used by its possessor to further any purpose he chooses, whether commercial, political or religious, regardless of whether it is judged moral or immoral.

For this reason, the over-riding ethic of scientists is that all scientific information is to be freely published: access is, in principle, available to all. This universal communism of knowledge soon brings scientists into conflict with representatives of sectional interests, including managers, who wish to preserve newly discovered forms of power from their competitors.

In the social sciences and management studies things have not reached that stage, chiefly because no one has discovered how to do anything new, or for that matter worked out what sort of thing they ought to discover. This leaves an open field for moralists, who proceed to confuse the issues to such an extent that the idea of science disappears. One psychologist promotes determinism, another advocates freewill. One management author preaches sustainability while another teaches pragmatism. One author promotes Christian values and another endorses the prescriptions of Machiavelli. In other words, they are frequently animated by personal value judgements and ever ready to point us towards the path of greater righteousness.

To define a management problem as a moral problem is to imply that managers could eliminate it by choosing to do so; and this implies that they already know how to do so: that the remedy is within their power. If this were true, managers would have no need of trying to develop a social science: they could already solve all the problems that worry moralists. If one believes that management problems can be eliminated by persuading people to make the requisite moral choices then one should remove oneself from management and join a seminary.

Like the social sciences, management studies are about reaching an effective understanding of the interdependencies which make society. This knowledge would allow managers to predict the unintended effects of intended changes with some accuracy and would open up the possibility of controlling, with the assistance of other groups, certain features of society – such as crime – which are products of the way the interdependencies are arranged. Any science has as its aim and function the achievement of control over events not now under human control; it has the hard task of extending our powers of control beyond what is now responsive to human choice.

The management training situation is quite plain. When HR managers, psychologists and trainers allow themselves to become evangelists for social reform they betray their vocation. Their example is soon followed by their colleagues who take to talking of events in terms of whether they should or should not be allowed to happen regardless of whether such control is within our powers. The problem of distinguishing between what changes it is within our power to make, and what states of affairs are determined by factors beyond our present control, simply disappears because it is assumed that nothing social is beyond our control. History and current affairs both mock this attitude but it proves difficult to counter and it exposes the weaknesses in management education and training and indeed in all the social sciences – the inability to come to grips with any way of identifying precisely what is determined by forces other than human choice.

7

The Leadership Myth

Charisma: Gift of grace: possessed by miracle workers who generally die young; misapplied to managers and politicians.

Rulers throughout history have wanted to believe that others obeyed them, not because they had the power to enforce obedience, but because they were 'born leaders'. This myth was invented by Plato and has been so successful that it is still debated seriously in business schools. In *The Republic*, Plato called the story of the 'born leader' the great lordly lie and advised rulers to use it to legitimise their power. He argued that with the help of one audacious lie rulers may, if they are lucky, persuade even themselves. It seems that politicians, bureaucrats and managers have been persuaded since for more than fifty years they have been obsessed with leadership. Their fascination with leadership is based on a desire, rarely stated openly, to believe that their power derives from subordinates' recognition of their exemplary personalities.

The way in which the notion of leadership has been used by psychologists and management consultants in industry and government has been well documented by Loren Baritz in *The Servants of Power*. He argued that the early formulations insisted that leadership was an art, something vague and even mystical that could not be reduced to scientific investigation or communicated to managers. According to this view, leaders are born and not made, a view which is closely related to the popular idea that leadership is a function of personality. Leaders were thought to have strong characters, self-confidence, sensitivity, integrity and imagination. This contradicted research which showed that about half of successful executives have volatile tempers and do not know, like or care about their colleagues. It was not until after the Second World War that managers embraced the view that authoritarian leadership in management was likely to fail since the consent of the managed was essential to success. Subordinates needed to be persuaded rather than ordered to behave appropriately. Power was not to be used where persuasion might work. And persuasion meant the ability to convince workers of the wisdom of management decisions. According to Baritz, this concern with leadership became a fetish after the 1950s. Conferences were dominated by the topic and speeches regularly emphasised the need to transform management into leadership. Managers liked to think that subordinates obeyed them because they were 'gifted visionaries', not because they had power to enforce obedience. In short, out of the desire of managers to be respected as persons rather than as powers grew an industry which continues to go from strength to strength. Leadership remains one of the most popular topics on the management training circuit and psychologists continue to write books about the personalities of leaders.

It is obvious that the leaders of the twentieth century had different personalities and were, alas, human-all-too-human. Indeed, their emotional instability and deficiencies as human beings encourage us to wonder how Stalin and Hitler became leaders. Management writers on leadership avoid such unsavoury characters and offer sanitised descriptions of the lives of their heroes. Many, however, continue to subject readers to lists of leadership 'traits' in spite of the fact that personologists have singularly failed to produce any meaningful results. The personality trait approach to the study of leadership – based on inferences from leader behaviour – faces the challenge of explaining the behaviour of followers, and it runs into insuperable problems.

The search for stable and enduring personal qualities of leaders has failed, and must fail, because leaders cannot be understood apart from the relationship with their followers. Both must be considered partners in the game of leadership and it is invalid to analyse one party at the expense of the other: leaders cannot exist without followers. But what is the basis of this relationship?

Melbourne academic W J Byrt began his book on leadership by rejecting the personality approach defended by Sir William (later Lord) Slim, a distinguished soldier and Governor-General of Australia. In a 1957 lecture for the Australian Institute of Management – *Leadership in Management* – Slim argued that leadership was a projection of personality: courage, will-power, knowledge, judgement and 'flexibility of mind'. He drew a distinction between leadership and management. Leadership, he argued, is of the spirit, compounded of personality and vision and its practice is an art. Management, on the other hand, is of the mind, more a matter of accurate calculation of statistics, of methods, time-tables and routine and its practice is a science. His final words to his audience were: 'Infuse your management with leadership, then they will show their mettle in the workshop as they have on the battlefield. Like me, they would rather be led than managed. Wouldn't you?'

Byrt presents Slim's lecture as an example of the conventional wisdom about leadership. And so it is. He noted that while it was not a great speech, it has been used extensively in many

Australian management development programmes. I remember attending management development courses in the early1980s in which Slim's ideas were treated as the last word on managerial leadership. Byrt summed up the conventional view as follows: 'It consists of influence over a person or group of persons who are inferior to the leader in some way: in status, ability or personality. A leader should possess certain qualities although there is little agreement on these. Some lists of qualities are so lengthy as to constitute an absurdity: few persons, if any, would possess all those stipulated.'[1] Byrt rejected the conventional view, based on personality, and defined leadership as a process whereby the behaviour of the led is *influenced* by a leader. He accepted the widely-held view that the leadership relationship is based on influence: leaders influence people.

'Leader' derives from 'laedare' which means to lead people on a journey. The concept carries the assumption that followers *choose* to accompany the leader on his travels and this assumes that there is no conflict of interest between the parties. Obviously, these assumptions cannot be said to apply to all super – and subordinate relationships. Managers have coercive power over their subordinates and it is naive to believe that the latter freely choose to follow the former. Authors who depend on the general relationship of 'influence' fail adequately to consider the power relationships involved in hierarchical relationships and the diverse ways in which people follow others, most of which are not examples of leadership.

The main problem is that, in trying to work with the relational concept of 'influence', authors cast their nets too wide. When we start calling managers and bureaucrats leaders there is no line of demarcation between those who influence others because of the position they occupy and those who influence others because of their exemplary personal qualities. We can be influenced by others in various ways (positively or negatively, voluntarily or involuntarily), and we follow others for diverse reasons (traditional, legal, technical). By relying on 'influence' as the fundamental relationship between leader and followers, many management writers fails to acknowledge cases where a conflict of interest exists between the parties and where it does not. This would seem to be an important issue where individuals are influenced coercively by people in positions of power, compared with those whose influence is personal and benign. That, say, Alfred Sloan and Jack Welch were capable managers is clear: that they were leaders is not.

When authors enumerate the choices confronting a student of leadership – a choice between the study of leaders and the study of followers – they give the impression that these are, methodologically, viable alternatives. They are not. The leader/follower dichotomy is false and it is not a viable method for the study of leadership. The only viable prospect for studying leadership is the relational approach favoured by social psychologists. Here one chooses to regard the relationships between leader and followers as the objective element in the picture. At first blush this seems unpromising as a scientific strategy because the very words used to name these relationships are unavoidably abstract and lack the kind of physical referent commonly associated with science. Unlike personologists, social psychologists have argued that the key to the puzzle of how to be scientific about individuals and society, leaders and followers, managers and subordinates, lies in regarding these relationships as the primary reality. According to this perspective, a relationship once named refers to an irreducible element in the researcher's conceptual scheme. There is no way in which the relationship between leaders and their followers can be analysed in terms of component relationships. Leadership stands for a relationship; it is not the sum of leaders' personalities. We may, of course, make inferences about the personalities or motivational states of individual leaders and their followers from the way the relationship manifests itself, and these inferences can be used as explanations for particular cases of leadership. It is also true that leadership overlaps with other relationships between the parties, such as conformity, obedience, influence, power and authority. But all of these may be present and leadership absent. So a relationship correctly identified can be regarded as irreducible, and this gives it valid status as a scientific starting-point.

If we persist with the view that 'influence' is the key relationship underpinning leadership we are faced with the difficult, if not impossible, task of deciding who are leaders and who are not. I suggest, therefore, that the key relationship underpinning leadership is *authority*. Because many authors fail to undertake an adequate conceptual analysis of the relationships between influence, power and authority, their selection of leaders is unconvincing. For example, there is a tendency nowadays to refer to celebrities as leaders. Of their fame and influence there can be no doubt. But it is not clear why celebrities should be called leaders: not clear until one realises that by defining leaders as those who influence a large number of people celebrities qualify. But someone has to *authorise* an individual as a leader. The notions of influence and authority are thus confounded. This is especially important given the difficulties facing researchers who try to separate a leader's personal influence from his positional power.

What does it mean to talk of a leader 'influencing' the behaviour of followers? For example, is a causal relationship assumed? If so, a power relationship must apply – so that any case in which the behaviour of person A is affected by person B is an instance of the power of B over A. But many writers assume that for this power to exist it has to be accepted (or authorised) by followers (otherwise they would not qualify as followers). The quandary which then arises can be expressed thus:

(a) leader power is equivalent to cause; (b) its operation requires the consent of the persons operated upon (followers); hence, by deduction, (c) followers must consent before a leader may cause anything to happen to them. The absurdity of this conclusion attests to the falsity of the premises. It is of the essence of power, as it operates upon people, that their consent is irrelevant. Where a person's consent is relevant, the situation has moved beyond power to authority. By relying on the general term 'influence' authors obscure the important differences between power and authority. A failure to set up conceptual distinctions between influence and power means that the issue of conflict of interest is by-passed. Where no conflict of interest between the parties exists influence is not regarded as power, for such activities as inducement and encouragement are then simply what the terms suggest. But where a conflict of interest does exist such activities are defined as manipulation and regarded as cases in which the terms 'influence' and 'power' are synonymous. Where a conflict of interest exists and either force or coercion comes into play, power of a kind not classified as influence is present.

In the study of leadership it is important to identify power independently from influence. Followers may be influenced by anything and everything about a leader, including his habits, manners, actions and rhetoric, whether or not these are directed at influencing them. That seems to be incontrovertible. But it is not the same as saying that what is influencing followers is the leader's power. Followers may be quite correct in believing that a leader has certain powers and may be suitably impressed; but they may be equally impressed when their beliefs about the leader's power are in fact false. On the other hand, a leader may make every effort to influence followers psychologically and fail completely, even if his powers extend to beating them to death. Even at this extreme it can be said that followers are influenced by the leader since they do something (die) that they would not otherwise do. Obviously, the extent of confusion that can be engendered by conflating two such terms is infinite.

Power can, and does, bring about significant change. An individual's personal power may be used in unauthorised ways. This may occur within a formal organisation but is more usually found outside it (e.g. crime). A state of affairs in which personal powers were not bounded by authority would, accordingly, be a state of barbarism. The movement towards a civil state is characterised by success in the struggle to bring power and its exercise under the moderating control of authority. This involves profound social and psychological developments: social because consensus has to be achieved as to which actions are morally acceptable; psychological because individuals have to control themselves according to these rules.

Power and authority must also be distinguished. The power exercised by leaders is dependent on their abilities to mobilise the activities of their followers and this is, in turn, dependent on the extent to which followers concede authority to them. The power attributed to leaders, therefore, is conditional on the concession of authority and is defined and circumscribed by these concessions. While leaders have the power to influence people because of their communications, their communications are successful insofar as they are judged to be authoritative. The assent of the people to whom a communication is addressed is a necessary condition for the establishment of it as authoritative, and if this is to occur certain conditions must be met. It must be such that followers understand it, believe it to be consistent with the purposes of their group, and believe it to be compatible with their personal interests. Authority, therefore, is a quality of a communication by virtue of which it is accepted. In the case of political, bureaucratic and managerial authority, it is a quality of a communication that is capable of *reasoned communication*. And reasoning means the willingness and ability to *argue* about relevant issues. Arguing is not, however, a necessary condition of leadership and is often not a feature of it at all.

Authority, then, refers to a relationship between persons or between person surrogates (e.g. institutional positions) and it is dissolved by dissent. Since authority implies more than a net advantage to individuals, it contains a *moral* element relating to the common good. Accordingly, it is sensitive to psychological factors. Power, on the other hand, does not require assent and its effects are not cancelled by dissent. Power is morally neutral and insensitive to psychological evaluation. Particular uses of power, by leaders for example, are morally evaluated and classed as being in accord with or counter to authority. The use by a leader of power that runs counter to authority may induce assent but not authority.

What, then, is the relationship between management and leadership? Do leaders get their following in the same way managers get theirs? Both management and leadership entail obedience. In the case of management it may be voluntary or involuntary, coercive or consensual. If this is true of leadership then there is no difference between the two concepts. If, however, we allow a difference between management and leadership, it would seem that leadership entails voluntary, but not involuntary, obedience.

German sociologist Max Weber can help us here with his analysis of management in modern capitalist societies.[2] Essentially Weber viewed capitalism as a form of social organisation based on the allocation of fixed duties to hierarchical positions. The duties are fixed through the introduction of general rules, often written regulations. Since this applies not only to the separate institutions of the state but to the state itself (in which the general rules take the form of laws), a high degree of concord can be developed between the state and its constituent institutions. So far as individuals are concerned, their job is specified in terms of routines designed to deal with the general case. The formal power to give the orders required for the carrying out of duties is distributed in a stable way and includes rules delimiting the coercive means at the disposal of officials. The hierarchy and the graded levels of authority generate a firmly ordered system of super – and subordination in which there is always a supervisor to every office (except the highest). Ideally the governed have the right of appealing against the decision of any office-holder to a higher authority, in a definitely regulated manner. Associated with roles are regulations specifying what must be done and what must not. The role specifications and the regulations then constitute the basis for the institution's claim that it has rationalised action, since by following them individuals should be able to serve the aims of the institution. Theoretically, they have no need to understand the purposes served by the organisation or to be able to judge whether any member's actions support it. They have merely to accept a very narrow responsibility – that of carrying out their own 'part' with precision and reliability.

Weber is explicit that bureaucracy is a machine and that it is an instrument in which people are merely functionaries. This impersonal character means that the mechanism – in contrast to structures based on personal loyalty – will readily work for anyone who knows how to gain control over it. The system specifies powers to be exercised by the person occupying each position in the organisation: formal power is made to cover the functions required in each office as exhaustively as possible. This power is attached to the *position* itself rather than to persons and is defined as explicitly as possible.

Weber's analysis leads, therefore, to the question of the difference between management and leadership, and on this issue there has been considerable debate. Since both management and leadership are based on authority, he reduced that problematic term to three 'ideal-types': 'charismatic', 'traditional' and 'legal-rational' authority.

Charismatic authority is based on a *person*, usually one who offers a solution to some very deep-seated and recalcitrant problem, and the solution offered is usually of a kind which both defines the problem more clearly than has been done before and gives the impression that the person offering it holds the key to understanding the central problems of existence. Charismatics are, therefore, leaders in the thousand-year tradition of the Anglo-Saxon word 'laedare'. Charismatics, it should be noted, are almost always assassinated. In Machiavelli's terms, they are unarmed prophets who always come to grief.

Traditional authority is well represented in the feudal system where person and position were usually connected by birth and there was a certain element of paternalism expected, so that the welfare of the inferior depended to some extent on the personal favour of the superior. Here, the inferior's estimate of the superior as a person could intrude on what was due to his position.

Legal-rational authority, in contrast, eliminates the personal and much of the uncertainty that goes with it and concentrates directly on whether a certain task gets fulfilled. Unlike traditional and charismatic authority, legal-rational authority is embedded in the social order. It extends to individuals only in so far as they occupy an organisational office and even then their powers are limited to a sphere of competence as defined within that social order. Obedience is due to individuals because they occupy a particular office and perform in their role with the appropriate technical competence. There is no other reason to obey their commands.

It is the merit of Weber's analysis that we can appreciate the difficulty in classifying as leaders managers, military officers, scientists and academics. Where the basis of managerial authority is legal-rational it is difficult to understand why managers, however effective they are, should be called leaders. While it is necessarily true that leaders need followers, most of the people we follow are not leaders. We follow policemen who direct us to the side of the road, but we do not call them leaders no matter how efficient they are. We follow the advice of qualified car mechanics but we do not call them leaders no matter how competent they are. And so it goes for politicians, managers, military officers, academics and bureaucrats. If we follow them, (and it is frequently a rational decision *not* to do so), it is for legal reasons, or because we judge them to be technical experts. Their status as *persons* is not important.

Charismatics are in a different category altogether, as Weber realised when he referred to them as leaders. In following a charismatic, individuals have to be prepared to suspend their critical judgements and invest considerable emotion in the person and his proposed journey. In matters of everyday life we don't need leaders. If we follow individuals it is because of the role they occupy and/or the technical skills they possess. In short, we follow technically competent individuals because it is rational to do so. But when we are faced with emergencies, with extraordinary needs, leadership is called forth. History teaches us that 'natural' leaders in moments of distress were neither appointed office-holders nor professionals but the bearers of specific gifts that were considered extraordinary – some were charismatic.

Authority may be conceded on the grounds that its possessor is knowledgeable about matters which are equally well known to many others, but such mundane authority is not to be equated with charisma. This includes a special feeling in the followers which goes beyond the mere recognition of superiority to include elements of awe, wonder, and even love. Charismatics persuade others of their ability to solve diverse problems, a power which suggests that they hold the key to some non-obvious feature of order in the universe.

The genuine charismatic, then, is seen as having a unique insight into cause-effect relationships hidden from other people, and this promises the solution of problems which have puzzled many. Since the existence of unsolved problems usually means that somebody is in difficulties, charismatics will often find their initial supporters among the socially powerful. The charisma of Napoleon was associated with his unexpected solution of the formidable military problems facing post-Revolutionary France, that of Adolf Hitler with his understanding of how National Socialism could be used to revitalise a depressed and demoralised people, and that of Jesus with his re-definition of the relationship between individual and group, and the new dignity it gave the former.

Historical figures having charismatic authority fall into two polar classes – military and religious. These are sharply distinguished by differing attitudes to power and authority. The military hero makes power a major tool in the solution of problems, and draws his following from among those who agree that power is the necessary and sufficient element for the solution of the problems being faced. The religious hero, in contrast, tends to avoid the use of power (unless miracles can be so classed) and attempts to work solely through authority. His following comes from among people who feel that power is a pointless acquisition unless the capacity to direct it wisely is in hand.

Some of the great charismatics have explicitly rejected power when it has been offered. These individuals wish their leadership to be unambiguously based on authority, involving personal consent of the led. They wish by their lives and actions to testify to the desirability and possibility of eliminating power as a basis for human relations and substituting understanding or, again where this fails, authority. If one wields no power, then there is no doubt whatever that those who follow one do so in freedom; if one does wield power there is no way whatever of determining whether people follow out of belief that the path chosen is correct or out of fear of consequences. If one uses power against those who challenge one's authority one immediately demonstrates that the claim of authority is partly hollow.

An even more remarkable fact about charismatics is the frequency with which they are killed by people whose established worlds they threaten to upset. This intense antagonism to charismatics appears as a puzzle in modern communities which consider themselves law abiding. Even democratic and popular politicians need bodyguards and the broader the authority conceded by followers the more serious the danger becomes. The very individuals who appear to be most cherished by their followers are the ones most exposed to its effects.

Charismatics often act in ways which deflect the hostility against them. They deny that their knowledge arises from their own powers and claim that it comes to them from God or some other supernatural source. This manoeuvre invites people to see them as having 'the spirit' and allows them to accept directions from them without intellectual jealousy. But it provides only temporary protection, for it soon becomes unmistakeable that the stream of successes and solutions emanates from one person, and the implication that this is due to his special personal powers becomes irresistible. The protection afforded by the claim of spiritual inspiration is also double-edged in that followers who admit such a possibility are free to ascribe it to either God or demons, and it is always permissible to destroy demons, or to incarcerate them in mental hospitals.

Weber argued that charisma is man's one chance of freedom, and the root source of social change. By his analysis it is the only element in society which enables a break-out from the routines which constitute bureaucracies. Even so, such breaches in tradition are temporary, for the followers of charismatics will strive to have their ideas and principles adopted – incorporated into a routinised social structure – and when they have been so absorbed, charisma dissipates.

Charisma is radically *opposed* to bureaucratic organisation because it is self-determined and sets its own limits. It is opposed to the economic infrastructure of bureaucracies and to their rules, roles and rewards. Charismatic leadership is naturally unstable because the mere fact of recognising the personal mission and extraordinary powers of charismatics establishes their status. They must perform heroic, miraculous deeds and should they cease to do so, their status and power evaporate.

If we choose to confine our study of leadership to charismatics the range of candidates is mercifully narrow. If we embrace the popular view that leaders are those individuals who influence large numbers of people, the range is very wide indeed. Furthermore, there is the question of the difference between effective and ineffective leaders.

Typically, authors of books on leadership state that they are not just interested in leadership, they are interested in *effective* leadership. In one sense 'effective leadership' is a pleonasm since the fact of leadership attests to its effectiveness, so that leadership cannot be ineffective. In another sense, 'effective leadership' means that the relationship is to be judged pragmatically by its consequences, and this is the sense in which managerial psychologists use the term. But pragmatic interpretations invariably suffer from problems of circularity – leaders are successful when they succeed. It is a truism that leaders achieve a degree of success and an historical fact that their effectiveness is, in many cases, short-lived. Is it accurate to say, for example, that Churchill was an effective leader in 1940 and an ineffective leader in 1945? Or was it the case that he was a leader in 1940 and he was not a leader in 1945? If a leader is defined as an individual who influences people then Churchill was a leader in 1940 and remained so until his death (since he significantly influenced a significant number of people every year of his life after 1940). The advantage of a pragmatic interpretation of leadership is that it enables psychologists to use the criterion of effectiveness after the event without modifying the status of a leader. So they can say that Churchill was effective in 1940 as a leader because of the effectiveness of his communications, and he was ineffective in 1945 *as a leader* because of the ineffectiveness of his communications. Circular reasoning of this type has haunted American pragmatic thinkers for more than a century. It is well known that pragmatists define truth as 'what works' and emphasise consequences rather than causes. When they claim that certain managers are leaders they rely on the pragmatic (and circular) argument that they became leaders because their behaviour 'worked' for them and their followers. But a theory which explains everything (after the event), can predict nothing (before the event). Pragmatists claim, in effect, that managers become leaders when their behaviour works for them and for others, but we only know that they are successful after they succeed. And it is managers themselves who determine what counts as success.

Managers are no longer uncontested figures. In recent years they are, as we say in Australia, decidedly 'on the nose'. Journalists call them 'bosses' and many people sneeringly refer to them as 'suits'. They are increasingly criticised for their refusal to acknowledge the moral nature of their activities and so the question of morality of ends, and therefore of management effectiveness in achieving those ends, is rarely discussed. We should not be surprised, therefore, that they try to legitimise themselves by appealing to their 'leadership qualities' or exemplary personalities. That managers want us to believe that they are leaders who will lead us on a journey to paradise would appeal to Plato and Machiavelli. But history tells us that leaders are likely to lead us to hell.

Managers cannot point to a set of abilities which enables them to predict causal relationships between organisational events. Without such abilities managerial authority evaporates since they cannot demonstrate that their moulding of organisations produces the results they claim. They are fortunate, however, to be able to take advantage of our habit of conceding authority to individuals when we believe them to have access to correct information to a degree which greatly exceeds our own. Naturally we do not concede authority lightly; and when we ascribe it to managers we have strict regard for the relationship between their standard of knowledge and that of those they are addressing. Thus we might recommend managers as authorities on business or bureaucracy, even if we have no intention of conceding that they know better than we do on certain matters which are in dispute between them and us.

The easiest way to qualify as an authority is to develop a high degree of personal competence in some restricted field of knowledge. This requirement places managers in a difficult position because they do not appear to have the sort of specialist knowledge that inspires confidence in their ability to manage people. Despite this, many people acknowledge their authority and obey them without hesitation. They may even go beyond this and accord managers authority about other matters also. But when they do this they are more liable to err.

When we concede managers authority on the grounds of personal competence, it is sometimes because we believe that they have superior knowledge of the means to desired ends. This is not the same as moral authority. The question of effective means is an amoral question requiring only a technical answer. Even so, we are not necessarily able to test the correctness of such technical answers with final precision.

Consequently we may well make errors in our ascription of personal competence.

Even when conceded on adequate grounds, personal authority has important deficiencies from the point of view of those interested in the direction of social power. It is both limited and impermanent. Mortal authorities grow old and senile and die. And even at the height of their powers, human beings are not able to maintain the large number of intense personal relationships that are required before personal authority can be fully conceded. This small span of authority means that organisations which depend on personal authority must remain small or expand through the concession of authority at second-hand – on hearsay evidence. Small groups have some advantages over large organisations, for managers are under the immediate scrutiny of their followers, and the group can remain highly sensitive to personal intelligence, direction and desire. But there are some tasks for which large-scale organisation is necessary or advantageous and personal authority then becomes inadequate. This problem is partly solved by the transfer of authority from persons to positions. This transfer calls for some means of attaching to the position precise directions for how to direct the actions of others. Where conditions necessitate the generation of social power on a large scale, reduction of dependence on personal authority is a requisite. The technique for doing this lies in refining the network of rules attached to the position and specifying the minimum technical qualifications required.

Authority, then, is always related to a class of action or information which is thought to be *right*. The rightness in question is sometimes moral and sometimes technical and much ambiguity is generated by the two possible usages. Some of the facets of authority depend on ascribing rightness to a person; some are cases in which authority is ascribed to an organisational role. Some kinds of authority change into others with apparent ease. The insight of the prophet becomes the dogma of the priest; the competence of the activist becomes the regulation of the bureaucrat. The direction of such change seems to lead to the accumulation of traditions or written instructions for right action; but once formed, such conventions show resistance to still newer ideas, and once firmly entrenched in an institutional form their replacement is often very difficult. Thus institutions are inherently conservative.

Australians who enter the field of management face a dilemma, indeed a paradox. As they attempt to manage by performance they find themselves confronted by a wall of resistance built upon local values. The danger is that the anti-authoritarian sentiment is exaggerated to include a generalised anti-authority attitude in which *all* authority figures are resisted. The paradox is that Australian managers need the authority to exercise power on behalf of their organisations, but are caught up in a postmodern society which has become more disdainful about authority generally. While it is rational to resist authoritarian managers, it is decidedly irrational to resist authoritative ones. The challenge for managers, therefore, is to convince others and themselves that they are indeed authoritative. And history shows us that, in Australia, this is no easy challenge to meet.

8

The RSI Debacle

Pain: Absence of pleasure. Maximised in blue-collar workers; minimised in management.

In Australia in the 1980s large numbers of working people complained of pain, generally in the wrist. They were told that they were suffering from Repetition Strain Injury (RSI), later to be re-named Retrospective Supplementary Income by those of a more cynical bent. RSI was an example of the progressive medicalisation of work behaviour in which notions of 'illness', 'treatment' and 'patient' figure prominently. The RSI phenomenon – or debacle – can be used as a case study of the tendency in Australian occupational health circles to emphasise medical rather than moral behaviour at work. This tendency, stimulated by professional interests, has retarded work reform strategies which aimed to increase autonomy for all working people.

One of the goals which guided work reform strategies in the Western democracies since the 1970s was autonomy for all workers. Scandinavian experiments with semi-autonomous work groups and the re-design of offices and factories were widely viewed as important steps in this direction. While work reform strategies in Australia were much discussed in the 1970s – especially job enrichment programmes and industrial democracy – Australian work environments showed little evidence of progress in these directions. Furthermore, managers and trade unionists tended to psychologise employment relations, exemplified by the myth of 'the careless worker' who caused unnecessary accidents, and the myth of the 'chronically dissatisfied worker' who caused unnecessary tension. The habit of looking to the personality of employees rather than factors in the work environment as explanations of work problems was especially characteristic of Australian managers in the 1980s and remains so to this day. The popularity of personality tests and training courses which focus on personality, motivation and now, emotional intelligence, illustrates and supports this contention.

As we have seen, Australian managers have long embraced the idea that performance has to be weighed against personality factors if working people are to 'get on with each other'. A consequence of managers concerning themselves with the personalities of their colleagues is that, sooner or later, they will be forced to deal with psychological as well as practical problems. If psychological problems are related to work activities, and if individuals adopt a Druckerian approach to management, they do not need to involve themselves in the internal workings of their colleagues' psyches. However, this is not the path Australian managers chose to follow. On the contrary, they actively turned their attention away from the work environment (which was the primary concern of trade union officials) toward the inner life of their colleagues. Involving themselves in psychological matters may not have been a sound move for managers but it was a godsend for management consultants, especially psychologists. Theories of motivation, personality, leadership, communication and team-building, proliferated while concurrently managers were required to undertake personality and intelligence tests to determine person-organisation 'fit'.

Relations between working people, like all human relations, are fraught with difficulties, especially where they are based explicitly on power relationships. Understandably, Australian managers work hard to minimise the effects of the overt application of power by a variety of means, including the myth that the workplace is a home away from home where work relations are treated as quasi-family relations. This has the obvious consequence that managers are quasi-parents and their subordinates are quasi-children. If accepted, this paternalistic strategy euphemises workplace language and disguises the reality of managerial power. Since one form of paternalism leads easily to other forms, it is inevitable that managers/parents become embroiled in the illnesses of their subordinates/children.

Clearly, subordinates in power relationships express their discontents in more covert ways than do managers. Thus, subordinates often use metaphors and symbolism to communicate their dissatisfaction. In Christian societies, one way to express discontent symbolically is to claim that one is unwell, in pain or ill. Responses to such claims are not supposed to be hostile or indifferent so that people who adopt the role of *sick patient* are considered to be acting honestly and ethically. In short, complaining of feeling unwell is a gesture calling forth a positive response from another person. This is what qualifies the relationship as moral since issues of right and wrong behaviour are involved, especially on the part of the person who responds to the 'sufferer'. The last word has to be put in quotes because it is possible that a person who complains is not in fact unwell, but is seeking support, attention, affection, love or some other reward. The point is that since we cannot experience the state of well-being of others, we infer it from their behaviour and words. A complaint about a sore neck might be a legitimate expression of a pain in the neck or it might be a lie, giving another meaning to 'pain in the neck'.

If moral conflicts are treated on their merits, issues of right and wrong are worked through, if not to resolution, at least to an understanding of the underlying problems involved. It is a cliché that complaints about a leaking tap are often symbolic expressions of more serious complaints (about money, supervisors, etc.); they are symbolic expressions by people in subordinate positions because overt complaints may result in unacceptable retaliation from those with more power.

However, if moral conflicts are re-defined so as to invalidate issues of right and wrong, those who complain of problems are likewise invalidated. One effective way to disarm critics is to declare them mentally ill and thus invalidate their complaints. For example, Stalin despatched large numbers of Soviet dissidents to the Gulag, labelling them as 'schizophrenics'. Similarly, when black Americans escaped from their chains, they were not treated as human beings who had moral grievances, but as organisms who were suffering from an illness called drapetomania, a 'medical condition' invented in the US and applied only to slaves who attempted to escape to freedom.

One way to deprive people of freedom and responsibility is to treat the moral conflicts in which they are involved as medical conditions for which they are not responsible and which require treatment. Policies and practices which treat moral dilemmas (behaviourally manifested) as if they are illnesses (physically or psychiatrically manifested) deprive individuals of their autonomy and create a therapeutic paternalism where people are 'demoralised', i.e., they are regarded as medical patients rather than moral agents.

In Australia legal cases have involved the 'demoralising' and medicalising of conflicts at work. In *Anderson Meat Packing Company versus Giacomantonio*, a worker was judged to be incapacitated for work while 'demoralised' after 'seeing' God in the cool room of the meat-works.[1] The use of the word 'demoralised' is surely significant because it suggests that people who report distress at work may lose their capacity for rational, and thus moral, behaviour and so cannot be considered responsible agents. In this way a moral issue – a man wanted to get out of the cool room – is medicalised.

Pain and discomfort have long been recognised as occupational hazards. For decades medical practitioners have noted the prevalence of simple muscle complaints among process workers. Medical intervention was rarely required and the problems were usually overcome by rest and prevented by uncomplicated changes to work practices and appropriate training. In a small minority of cases the problems were diagnosed as tenosynovitis, which had been associated with work activity and relieved by conservative medical treatment. Researchers advised all parties to consider the influence of psychosocial factors both in and beyond the workplace because these were important in the incidence, persistence and prevention of such complaints.

In 1976 an industrial health group at the Liverpool Women's Health Centre in Sydney, published a booklet *You Job: His Profit or Your Life* which provided information on tenosynovitis. The following year a Workers' Health Centre was established at Lidcombe (NSW) and a Workers' Health Action Group in Melbourne. These centres were influential in drawing attention to 'repetitive injuries' as a serious occupational health issue since more than half the workers treated at workers' health centres suffered from what was later called Repetition Strain Injury (RSI). In an article entitled 'A Crippling New Epidemic in Industry' published in *New Doctor* in 1979 these 'injuries' were attributed to the inadequacies of the medical profession and legal/compensation policies and practices.

Prior to the late 1970s RSI was unknown in occupational medicine. Government compensation statistics showed that the number of musculoskeletal disorders had been relatively static for many years. Statistically, the RSI 'epidemic' commenced around 1979 and continued well into the 1980s when it sharply declined. The increases could not be explained by changes in the size or composition of the workforce, the nature of work processes, or the way official statistics were compiled. In NSW, for example, the number of musculoskeletal cases increased from 670 (1976–7) to 4550 (1983–4), an unparalleled increase. By 1983–4 RSI represented 28.5 per cent of total cases in NSW compensation statistics. Females accounted for about 65 per cent of claims which partly reflects the proportion of females in jobs that involve repetitive tasks. It remains to be tested whether females engaged in repetitive tasks are more likely than males to act like patients.

Large organisations, particularly in the public sector, recorded similar increases. Unofficial estimates placed the national total in excess of 20,000 and almost 4000 cases were recorded in Australian Government organisations in the December 1985 quarter alone. The incidence pattern was, however, inconsistent with exposure to repetitive tasks. Some organisations remained unaffected whereas others, including Telecom, with similar work patterns reported outbreaks of 'epidemic' proportions. Of those organisations massively affected some revealed a pattern which suggested a contagion effect in that workers were affected in quick succession.

Clearly, Australians in the 1980s were involved in an epidemic – of compensation claims. But what were people seeking claims for? Did the extraordinarily rapid rise in claims correspond to an underlying incidence of musculoskeletal injuries? Or was the epidemic one of mass hysteria? Or was it mass malingering?

Historically and unsurprisingly, workers' compensation cases recorded under the classification 'Synovitis, Bursitis, Tenosynovitis' generally affected blue-collar, factory workers. But by the early 1980s a new incidence pattern emerged. No longer were these injuries exclusively associated with semi-skilled workers on production lines. Keyboard operators and clerical workers in traditionally 'safe' white-collar jobs began reporting these injuries in increasingly large numbers. As claims for compensation mounted and test cases were decided in favour of the complainants, insurance premiums skyrocketed.

In the early 1980s researchers at the Australian Council of Trade Unions (ACTU) were collecting data on tenosynovitis, cervico-brachial injury and what the Workers' Health Centre in NSW called 'repetitive movement injuries'. The ACTU issued guidelines in August 1982 in which the major author, John Mathews, coined the term 'repetitive strain injury' to widen the scope from 'movement' to 'strain' incurred at, say, a poorly designed keyboard. Mathews was influenced in his thinking by white-collar jobs with new computer-based word-processing systems in the Australian Taxation Office, where word-processing targets of 12,000 keystrokes per hour, without rest breaks, were common. The purpose of the ACTU recommendations was to encourage unions to negotiate limits on repetitive activity and regular breaks. The unions were spectacularly successful in having these demands met. The front line in this endeavour was to be the unions' elected safety representatives. It was Mathews' intention to have Australian workplaces peopled by worker representatives who would monitor conditions and ensure that employers were meeting their 'duty of care'. The ACTU guidelines were conceived, therefore, as guides for these workplace negotiations. Importantly, Mathews' document was critical of those who want to screen individuals medically to determine susceptibility to RSI. He noted that treating RSI medically yielded depressingly poor results.[2]

National concern about RSI and its costs to the community resulted in the Australian Government establishing two independent enquiries which recommended substantial changes to

the design of work. Whereas earlier approaches to the prevention of RSI concentrated on biomechanical factors – posture,
speed, etc. – the RSI Committee report observed that this
approach was relatively ineffective since some organisations had
spent large sums of money on work-stations only to find that
the problem remained.

By 1986 RSI was known as 'Retrospective Supplementary
Income', 'Runaway Social Invention', 'Golden Wrist', 'Kangaroo
Paw'. It was listed in the 'International Classification of Diseases'
of the World Health Organization among the Somatoform
disorders which is a subset of mental and behavioural disorders,
including writer's cramp, occupational neurosis and conversion
hysteria.

The RSI debate became acrimonious and speakers at public
forums were frequently abused and threatened, as I can attest
from personal experience. Critics of the orthodox medical interpretation were accused of supporting insurance companies and
of gross insensitivity to the suffering of their fellow citizens.
Out of this often ill-tempered debate four perspectives emerged, although only three were widely discussed in public forums
and professional articles.

The medical perspective dominated the debate and the government commissions. RSI was assumed to be a medical condition
which can be diagnosed and treated. The injury is attributed to
biomechanical factors, such as inadequate work practices, which
must be rectified to prevent further injury. Injured workers are
treated conservatively (rest) or actively (physiotherapy, surgery).
This perspective was endorsed by the National Occupational
Health and Safety Commission but it slighted the influence of
psychosocial factors and gave RSI a medical legitimacy that was
unwarranted because of the absence, in the vast majority of cases,
of the necessary clinical signs which are needed for a valid diagnosis. The medical view was that RSI is a physical condition of

traumatic origin caused by biomechanical factors. It was widely promoted by medical practitioners even though they were not able validly to explain RSI's epidemiology or its distribution in the workplace.

The official opposition within the medical profession came from psychiatry. RSI is not a physical condition but a psychiatric one, probably conversion hysteria. Some psychiatric conditions closely mimic physical illness and have been known to occur en masse in industrial settings. Various psychological problems at home and at work cause psychological conflict which manifests in this symbolic disorder. Consequently, complainants require psychotherapy to resolve their personal problems. This perspective was promoted by several psychiatrists, orthopaedic surgeons and rheumatologists some of whom were employed by insurance companies to give evidence in legal proceedings. If RSI is a neurosis which is not occupational in origin, it is not compensable.

A third view was that RSI is neither a medical nor a psychiatric condition, but malingering. Most complainants are faking pain and cheating society. RSI, therefore, is a hoax consciously used (though not invented) by workers to gain rewards. This perspective caused a public furore because it simultaneously impugned the motives of workers and the diagnostic skills of the medical profession. It was widely discussed in the media and defended by anonymous authors.

Leigh Deves and I defended a fourth perspective.[3] RSI can be characterised as a social movement based on a system of rewards applied to people who *complain* of pain (and other discomforts – tingling, weakness) at work. Consequently, people who are essentially healthy but experience pain choose to complain about pain rather than adopt a stoical attitude thereto. Defenders of this perspective were labelled 'social constructionists' and dismissed because it was claimed that they, or their arguments, supported insurance companies in their efforts to blame the victims and avoid paying workers' compensation. They did not.

While these four perspectives cannot be reconciled because they differ on fundamental assumptions about the causes and nature of RSI, the one theme which links them is that of pain and the *reporting* of pain. The reporting of pain is intimately bound up with the role of 'patient', just as the treatment of pain is bound up with the role of doctor. One may adopt the patient role with or without pain, just as one may treat a person who has or does not have pain.

The accepted medical criterion for diagnosing illness is the presence of a physical *sign*, (i.e. a demonstrable physico-chemical alteration of the body), with or without *symptoms* (e.g. experiences of pain). The notion of RSI derives its main support from known medical conditions, such as tenosynovitis or carpal tunnel syndrome, with which it is erroneously equated. A condition like tenosynovitis is diagnosed by its signs (e.g. inflammation) and symptoms (e.g. pain). In the majority of cases of RSI, however, (perhaps as many as 90 per cent according to some researchers), diagnosis is made on symptoms alone, i.e., on the basis of a communication or complaint.

The idea of RSI is thus firmly based on *complaining*, unlike established diseases which are based on independent medical signs. Symptoms without signs are communications not diseases, complaints not 'conditions', until proven otherwise. The fact that medical diagnoses are made on the basis of symptoms alone does not mean they are valid, or responsible.

Critics challenged this argument claiming that: 'Spillane and Deves support this position by arguing that where symptoms exist, without physical signs, they should not be treated as diseases but rather as complaints or communications. This argument is based largely on uncritical acceptance of the familiar claim that where medical practitioners are unable to identify physical signs of injury it cannot be presumed to exist . . . It is also possible that medical practitioners really lack the diagnostic skills or the technology to identify the signs. Spillane and Deves overlook this possibility and, after noting claims, (disputed elsewhere), that up to 90 per cent of diagnoses of RSI rely on reports of subjective symptoms, they conclude that the assumption that RSI pain arises from repetitive movement at work "is unwarranted on the evidence".[4]

Never was a challenge so easily met. The critics were clearly confused about diseases and their diagnosis. In the Western medical tradition the fundamental axiom is that diagnoses of disease are based on *signs*. Historically, if people who complained of pain or discomfort in the wrist were found to have physical signs – say inflammation – they were probably diagnosed with tenosynovitis. In the case of RSI, the majority of diagnoses were based on symptoms alone since there were no signs. It is of course true that medical practitioners often base their putative diagnoses on symptoms alone. In the absence of signs, however, diagnosticians can at best suggest possibilities. They may be right or they may be wrong. But they cannot maintain the position that medicine is objective and scientific while basing their diagnoses on subjective criteria – their impressions or inferences. Putative diagnoses are not real diagnoses and putative illnesses are not real illnesses. While the public is frequently told what medical practitioners and experts 'believe' or 'assume' to be the facts about conditions like RSI (or ADHD, depression, schizophrenia, bi-polar disorder and a host of other 'conditions' diagnosed on the basis of symptoms alone), their beliefs or assumptions are *not* facts. At law people are presumed innocent until proven guilty; in medicine people are assumed healthy until proven ill. That doctors or their apologists diagnose medical and psychiatric illnesses without evidence represents another manifestation of 'medical mugging'.

RSI was based on complaints of pain (or discomfort). Clearly, one person cannot experience another person's pain. Pain cannot be observed directly, although it is often inferred from a person's communications: the experience of pain is private and the expression of pain is public. When people say they have pain we may believe them because they appear to be distressed, or we may choose to believe that they are pretending to have pain for some unstated reason. The point is that we can only guess. We may seek reasons to support our belief – their history of physical illness, their tendency to complain or act stoically, the logic and politics of the situation they find themselves in, and so on. Furthermore, our own value system may tend to predispose us to believe they are ill or malingering. Logically, then, since pain and discomfort are subjective experiences, unlike epileptic convulsions, the actual incidence of malingering in conditions like RSI (and mental illnesses generally) can never be known.

When people experience pain they can communicate it, complain about it, or conceal it. Those who complain of pain may go on to define themselves as patients. A person can experience pain but choose not to be a patient. Or a person can choose to be a patient without the experience of pain. Since people generally act as they are rewarded, and if complaining of pain is rewarded, some (and in the case of RSI, many) people will choose to become patients (with or without pain).

Alternatively, some people who are treated by doctors and psychiatrists as patients do not suffer from an illness and do not want to be patients. When people with pain are told that they may be in the first stage of a crippling disease which demands urgent medical treatment, both illness and patient role are applied to the experience of pain. Furthermore, turning people into patients exposes them to a medical/legal game which few understand or escape from happily. If they are not labelled as sick patients they risk being labelled as mentally ill or malingerers. It was difficult in the 1980s to adopt a humane approach to this problem when workers claimed managers made them ill and managers retaliated with company doctors, psychiatrists, lawyers and accusations of malingering.

Pain is an inexorable aspect of the human condition and the causes of much chronic discomfort remain a mystery. When people suggest possible causes of their discomfort the responses they encounter from family, friends and doctors influence their subsequent behaviour. When working people with pain complain about their working conditions and their views are ignored or criticised some choose to communicate their dissatisfaction by becoming patients. Where the work climate encourages medicalising work behaviour or rewarding illness, some people are easily induced to become patients. Thus morals are confused with medicine, values with valium.

RSI was a social movement and not a medical epidemic. It was characterised by a significant increase in the number of people who, in the absence of diagnosable signs, chose to become, or were defined by others as, patients. Logically, though not empirically, it can be asserted that some experienced pain and others did not. While this logical conclusion is obvious, many people during the RSI era became angry at the very thought that anyone would suggest that some workers are malingerers. On the other side, some people took the unwarranted position that all, or the majority of, RSI complainants were cheats and malingerers. Sadly, logical reasoning was not a feature of the RSI debate.

Before the invention of RSI workers experiencing pain were neither encouraged nor inclined to adopt the helpless and dependent role of patient. And neither did they seek to use their discomfort politically, despite the availability of this line of redress, either because their problems were dealt with locally or they risked penalties for complaining. When, at the height of the RSI 'epidemic', Deves and I visited the US to enquire about similar experiences, the general response was that if workers complained of work-related pain they would be penalised. This left open the possibility that repetitive work was causing widespread problems which, for obvious reasons, went unreported. In American workplaces there were no incentives and severe penalties for becoming patients with pain. Rather than support the medical or psychiatric perspectives, however, this fact supports the conclusion that RSI was a social movement built on the attitudes to work and health adopted by the Australian community, especially its occupational health, legal and compensation arms.

In the 1980s the historical pattern changed from cooperation to confrontation. Warring parties sought the advice of medical and legal experts to justify an adversarial position. In the absence of clinical signs of physical illness, workers were accused of malingering or treated as mentally ill. Having had their motives impugned and personal experiences invalidated, workers retaliated through medical certification and many were removed from work for indefinite periods. Medical certification guaranteed them access to a compensation system which did not encourage recovery. Personal activity was discouraged because insurance companies employed private investigators whose evidence, admissible in industrial courts, could prove embarrassing to plaintiffs. Faced with the prospect of jeopardising their claims many workers adopted, or were placed in, a state of dependency leading to iatrogenic consequences, such as anxiety and depression. These secondary conditions led to further medical treatment or psychotherapy. Dependency was thus required and promoted through medical and legal intervention, which probably accounts for the persistence of symptoms beyond reasonable expectations.

RSI is not and never has been medically recognised for clinical purposes. The term is a residue constructed from differential diagnostic practice. According to the inventor of the term, my Macquarie University colleague John Mathews, it was never intended for use in legal proceedings. The ACTU's 1982 recommendations crossed an invisible line; the prevention of RSI was different from the prevention of occupational deafness where the physical cause was clear. How one *felt* became an issue for the courts.

That RSI gained widespread acceptance in medical and legal proceedings is the result of injudicious medical practices: RSI was consistently referred to as 'a crippling disease of epidemic proportions'. Managers' clumsy efforts to substitute malingering or mental illness served only to stiffen trade unionists' resolve to fight this 'illness' medically. Government reports compounded the problem by issuing codes of practice that failed to take account of psychological factors, even though researchers had emphasised their importance. For example, one of my studies showed that satisfaction with one's supervisor and control over one's work were better predictors of RSI complaints than were biomechanical factors.[5] Worse still, the guidelines provided by the National Occupational Health and Safety Commission, though ostensibly aimed at constructive work reform, resulted in establishing coercive work routines, standardising work, and scrutinising workers. These guidelines were almost the exact opposite of the work reform strategies and practices which emerged from occupational research during the 1970s which sought to maximise autonomy for all working people.

The legally sanctioned use of the medical model in Australian workplaces has led to the increased power of medical practitioners and psychiatrists to determine who is healthy and who is ill, and the increased dependency of those who adopt, or are allocated to, the role of patient. Given the predilection of doctors to diagnose conditions in the absence of clinical signs and to transform moral dilemmas into medical conditions, it is difficult to see an end to therapeutic paternalism.

The RSI 'epidemic', which represented a ten-fold increase in claims for compensation, has subsided. In the late 1980s trade unions modified their prevention campaigns while the Australian Medical Association and the Royal Australian College of Physicians criticised the concept of RSI and called for a new name. They got it. Unbelievably, RSI is now known as *Occupational Overuse Syndrome* which indicates that we have learned little from the 1980s. Bruce Hocking, one-time Medical Director at Telecom, provided convincing evidence that there was no relationship between RSI and technology or the ergonomics of the work station.[6] His research revealed that 83 per cent of complainants were female with younger age groups and part-time workers over-represented in the statistics. Among typists and computer operators, the fastest and busiest reported the *lowest* proportion of cases, a similar finding to that of the Departmental Committee into Telegraphists' Cramp in 1911. A much publicised legal case, *Cooper versus Commonwealth of Australia* (1987) was lost. Finally, the *Medical Journal of Australia* closed correspondence on RSI between 1988 and 1991, and then reactivated it in 1993.

In 1995 a consensus statement, published by the Australian Faculty of Occupational Medicine, attributed the causes of the RSI 'epidemic' to: technological change, poor management practices (failure to address workers' complaints); unions' increased attention to workers' health and safety (and compensation for work-related illness); the spread of RSI from blue – to white-collar workers and publicity about large compensation payouts (some of which were sensationalist and irresponsible); workers' discontent transformed into 'illness'; medical practitioners' confusion about diagnosis, pathogenesis, treatment and prognosis; RSI support groups that reinforced patienthood; government reports that enshrined a mechanistic model of RSI instead of considering psychological factors.

After the promulgation of the *Workers' Compensation Act* in 1987 large lump-sum payments through common law claims dropped dramatically in NSW. Claims for 'Occupational Overuse Syndrome' halved in the period 1995–6 and 1999–2000 and claims accepted decreased from 1333 to 179.

The medicalisation of work behaviour continues, however. In the 1990s RSI gave way to an even bigger 'epidemic' – occupational stress. Combining an insensitivity to language with an ignorance of the lessons learned from the RSI debacle, government authorities now refer to occupational stress as 'psychological injury' which, because of the word 'injury', ensures that it became a matter of legal disputation.

Stress costs around $1.3 billion per year in Australia and stress claims are increasing while other claims are decreasing. Between 1996–7 and 2003–4 claims for all injuries and illnesses decreased by 13 per cent while stress claims during that period increased by 83 per cent. In 2002–4 claims for 'psychological injury' accounted for 7 per cent of total workers' compensation claims but nearly 27 per cent of total costs of claims. Sydney psychiatrist Yolande Lucire has it right when she argued that when the occupational stress epidemic replaced the RSI epidemic in the early 1990s, the medical profession was poised to medicalise as psychological injury the consequences of abrasive and dysfunctional relationships, overwork and understaffing.[7]

Since many stress claims are based on moral problems, such as getting on with people at work by acting in appropriate ways, we need to rethink the issue of what constitutes an 'injury' and 'illness' and allow the possibility that we misuse these concepts at our peril. This is especially the case with 'psychological injury' which, as a substitute for 'stress', raises more problems than it solves.

9

Occupational Stress

*Stress: Overstressed feature of management life, but only in the
sense that managers impose it on others; the absence of which in
humans is found only in cemeteries; quasi-medical condition used
to avoid work. 'Stressed' is 'desserts' spelt backwards.*

Nietzsche believed that individuals who calculate the
value of each day according to their degree of happiness
are mere pawns in the game of life. Freedom, for Nietzsche,
meant becoming more indifferent to stress and hard work. He
promoted a philosophy based on energy, vitality and joyful
striving and had little time for those who complain of the stresses
of life. Nietzsche's tone – a product of the 1880s – is very different from the strident culture of complaint which characterised
Western society one hundred years later. Complaining about the
stress of life has become so acceptably widespread that it takes a
brave individual to adopt Nietzsche's philosophy and promote
it openly.

Fifty years later, Sigmund Freud argued that modern society
is characterised by 'civilised nervousness' and its dominant
expression is the complaint about the difficulties of living in the
modern era. The popularity of psychoanalysis in the twentieth

century is testimony to the ubiquitous nature of complaining and the determination to institutionalise it. The institutionalisation of complaining has been combined with the postmodern obsession with personal rights. Taken together and ignoring personal responsibilities a social movement built on stress has evolved which has assumed 'epidemic' proportions. Stress is no longer regarded as an important and inexorable part of life, and thus something to be valued. Rather, stress is nowadays regarded as a 'condition' to be treated, a 'symptom' of malaise, an infringement of one's rights, an assault upon one's psyche, a reason to engage in litigation, an example of coercion and harassment, a product of power politics, and an excuse for early retirement. Coupled with the assertion that we live in a rapidly changing world in which technology has overpowered sensitive people the stress movement has grown to uncontainable dimensions.

'Stress' is borrowed from engineering and many of those who foist the concept on the public claim the prestige of science in justification. When the stress on bridges is too great they collapse. So by analogy, when the stress on individuals is too great they collapse. A philosophy of mechanics is thereby introduced into psychology and from there to the workplace and law courts. Individuals are transformed into machines which respond positively or negatively to forces brought to bear upon them. Individuals are, therefore, defenceless in the face of external pressures which invade them, so to speak. Resistance is ultimately futile since individuals cannot be held responsible for their behaviour because they are, strictly speaking, not individuals at all. They have few or no choices when faced with external pressures and, after a certain point has been reached, collapse under their power. Where choice is not possible responsibility is not relevant. This minefield of confusions and contradictions has captured the public imagination to such a degree that anyone who claims that stress is good is regarded as not quite sane.

Clearly, not all stress is negative and harmful to personal health and well-being: the only place one can find people without stress is a cemetery. Without the energy or stress which derives from stimulation humans would lack the ability to solve practical problems and function effectively. Yet stress is widely regarded as a necessary evil. How did a universal human condition get such a bad reputation? Why do some people complain of stress while others thrive on it?

Before attempting to answer these questions it should be emphasised that there is no independent entity called 'stress' even though people talk and write about it as if it were a concrete noun. Stress is not, for example, a definable environmental noxious agent – indeed it is not objectively definable at all. 'Stress' is a relational term – a metaphor employed to describe particular interactions between individuals and their environments. For example, people who lack or lose control over important aspects of their environment are likely to describe their situation as 'stressful'.

Working with a difficult manager may lead to changes in bodily functioning (increased heart rate and hormonal secretions) and changes in feelings (tension and frustration). It is important to emphasise, however, that stressors cannot be abstracted from the individual's perception of them. This explains why a stressor produces an effort reaction for one person and distress for another. For example, researchers have found it difficult to demonstrate the harmful effects of noise because of the meaning attached to it; what is a source of musical pleasure for some is painful noise for others.

When interviewed about stress some people call on their powers of adaptability and endurance to deny that stress is important; they take the stand that one simply has to put up with stress for the sake of progress. Some are explicit about the view that those who complain about stress are neurotic, weak, unduly querulous or lacking in hardihood. Their attitude implies that they find some cause for pride in adapting: stress is something to be endured.

Some years ago I was a member of a research team of psychologists whose task was to investigate attitudes to aircraft noise. The team interviewed residents who lived directly under the aircraft flight path at Sydney airport. We wanted to know what the residents thought of living in an environment that was dominated by considerable, intermittent aircraft noise. Our first finding was that residents who lived further away from the flight path were more likely to refuse to be interviewed: they could see no reason to participate in the study since noise wasn't a problem for them. We therefore expected to hear more complaints about aircraft noise when we talked with residents closer to the flight path. Surprisingly, many residents under the flight path took the position that they simply had to put up with aircraft noise. Initially, we thought that this view was likely to be confined to those who worked with or around aeroplanes, but although this view was widely endorsed by such people, it was held by residents generally. Even though most of the residents admitted that aircraft noise was a nuisance, they took the view that it was something which could (and should) be endured. It did not press on them as immediately as their financial struggles. It was best ignored. Nevertheless, the research team believed there was something false about claims of imperturbability. The taped interviews contained cases where the effects of passing aircraft on conversation are plainly evident yet the residents said it bothered them not at all. This is the other side of the stress movement in which stoical responses disguise objective problems in living. For if most of the residents who were interviewed say they are not troubled by aircraft noise, and if these data are taken at their face value, they could be used to justify significant increases in air traffic or the building of airports near domestic residences.

Where individuals adopt the policy of calling on their powers of adaptation in this way they become unreliable instruments for measuring the fitness of the environment, particularly for others who are not so inured. It is exactly this psychological phenomenon which has permitted the progressive process which is described as destruction of the environment. Excessive reliance on interviews and attitude surveys carries the risk of pointing us toward environments which approach the limits of human tolerance rather than towards better conditions.

The individualistic nature of the stress response has also created problems for researchers who rely on attitude surveys which invite a variety of strategic responses. This is especially true of 'stress' and 'satisfaction' surveys which use questions that are general, impersonal and do not raise the need for specific action. Such questions invite uncritical replies. For example, the following questions produce highly positive responses:

– Do you believe that you are doing something useful?
– Are you able to talk freely with your boss?
– Do you feel accepted by people in your group?

Questions which produce less conservative responses are those which emphasise 'anticipation', of being deliberately prepared for future changes:

– Is the person affected by a change of job sometimes the last one to know about it?
– Do your managers need training in human relations?
– Do you think that managers are good at explaining the reasons for their actions?

These questions involve particular themes: clarification of organisational goals; information about on-going activities; education and personal development. When people are asked whether they are satisfied with their lives their responses are generally positive – a mixture of resignation and accommodation. When people are asked questions about the future, and what is needed to understand and anticipate it, responses will be less positive. Perhaps a concern for the future creates anxiety, or the thought of a future much like the present creates apprehension. It is one thing to resign oneself to the present but quite another to see this as the norm for the future.

Several researchers have sought an explanation for how some people live with high levels of stress but do not fall victim to premature illness. They insist on the importance of 'stress buffers', behaviour patterns which allegedly protect people who experience considerable stress from consequent illness. The idea is that some people cope with stress because they do not behave stressfully when many people do. There follows the circular conclusion that they do not react stressfully because they are resistant to stress. These people are called *hardy*. Now if stress exists as an independent entity, no one could escape it and coping would have to be employed to minimise its effects. If, on the other hand, stress does not exist as such, then some people will refuse to admit that they are stressed.

Some hardy researchers decided, however, that the 'hardy' types have something that the 'stressed' types lack – a hardy personality. Suzanne Ouellette-Kobasa developed a profile of the 'hardy personality' which is contrasted with the illness-prone personality. Hardiness consists of personal control (versus powerlessness), challenge (versus threat), and commitment (versus alienation). Hardy individuals involve themselves in whatever they are doing (commitment), act as if they can influence the events forming their lives (control), and consider change to be a stimulus to development (challenge). Ouellette-Kobasa argued that people develop hardy personalities if they have experienced in early life: considerable breadth and variety of events; stimulation and support for exercising the intellect; approval and admiration for doing things themselves; and people who act as role-models by advocating hardiness and demonstrating it by their actions. Her studies of American managers showed that those who experienced high levels of stress but did not report illness showed greater degrees of control, challenge and commitment than managers in whom similar stressful events were associated with much illness.[1]

As stress is a relationship between individuals and their environments it cannot be understood apart from that relationship. It is well known, for example, that personal performance is related to levels of environmental stimulation. The Yerkes-Dodson Law states that the relationship between performance and level of stimulation can be expressed graphically as an inverted U, which means that performance is maximised at a moderate level of stimulation. Since humans need adequate levels of stimulation to function effectively, too little stimulation is accompanied by feelings of boredom, apathy, inactivity and low levels of performance. This can be as unhealthy as excessive stimulation, as shown by the rapid deterioration of many people after retirement. At the other extreme, too much stimulation is accompanied by irritability and anger so that performance deteriorates and can, in extreme cases, lead to illness. While some people appear to thrive on excessive stimulation there is a point beyond which performance deteriorates and health is affected adversely.

If individuals need to have a moderately varied flow of experiences it follows that they also need to have a degree of control over their levels of stimulation. For example, people working in jobs which allow them to adjust levels of stimulation when they fall outside an acceptable range are less likely to report stress symptoms than those whose level of stimulation is beyond their control. Stress is not merely a problem of underload or overload – personal control must be taken into account.

Robert Karasek has pointed to the many contradictory findings in occupational stress research which can be traced to incomplete models derived from mutually exclusive research traditions.[2] One tradition emphasises job control and another job demands. Both traditions have to be analysed to avoid inconsistencies, such as the finding that both managers and assembly-line workers have stressful jobs, but the latter report higher levels of stress. One factor which might account for this difference is job control – the ability to moderate levels of demand. Karasek's studies of Swedish and American workers confirmed his prediction that people working in high demand and low control jobs would report the highest frequency of stress symptoms. Decreasing job demands alone is not an effective solution, however, since it leads to passivity and boredom. Workers in passive jobs reported the highest degree of non-participation in active leisure, demonstrating a 'carryover' from work to leisure and little evidence that deficiencies in the work environment are compensated for by choice of leisure activity. This finding has led some people to conclude that workers in passive jobs are a self-selected sample in that those with passive personalities are more likely to accept such jobs and remain in them. There is no convincing evidence to support this view, although it is widely entertained in management circles.

The lowest levels of stress symptoms and the highest levels of participation in social activity are found in people who work in jobs which offer high levels of control. Employees in low-discretion jobs with little opportunity to use creative talents report feelings of monotony, boredom and stress. These are more widespread and intense among employees who are young, well-educated and whose jobs are severely circumscribed as to variety, skill and social interaction.

The 1980s represented the halcyon days of occupational stress research in Australia. Rejecting questionnaire studies as crude and misleading, researchers used hormonal analysis to index the 'physiological cost' of work. Their research strategy was based on the following assumptions: there is a physiological cost attached to all jobs – in some cases the cost is high, in others low; this cost varies with the type of job and with individuals; this cost can be assessed independently of attitude or personality surveys by analysing 'stress' hormones – adrenaline, noradrenaline and cortisol. Numerous studies have shown that reports of anxiety and aggression are correlated with elevated levels of adrenaline and noradrenaline respectively. Feelings of depression, hopelessness and helplessness are related to elevated levels of cortisol and suppression of the immune response, suggesting possible relationships with particular illnesses. While it is not possible to say that a certain level of hormonal secretion is an indicator of distress that is harmful to the health of an individual, there is considerable evidence of an association between chronically elevated cortisol levels and the incidence of degenerative disease.

In an elegant study, Jack Bassett established that there are two stages in the stress-induced development of ischemic heart disease and that the hormones adrenaline, noradrenaline and cortisol have a mediating role in this process.[3] In the first stage the interaction of increased levels of these hormones leads to greater sensitivity of the heart. However, the sensitivity is not matched by the usual increase in dilation of the coronary arteries. At this point a functional but not a structural change has occurred. In the second stage there is a structural alteration to the arteries (coronary occlusion) which occurs when there have been repeated stress-induced increases in hormones. These repeated hormone increases lead to a number of changes in the arteries in both structure and function, culminating in coronary arterio-sclerosis.

Many jobs require people to maintain acceptable levels of performance under difficult conditions. Workers who achieve this goal do so at a cost which is reflected in the secretion of hormones. This is because adrenaline, noradrenaline, cortisol, heart rate and blood pressure increase as a result of attempting to maintain job performance under conditions of job overload and underload. Where performance is maintained under difficult conditions, physiological cost increases and this may be accompanied by stress reactions and, in the long-term, ill-health.

In 1979 psychologist George Singer and I spent a research sabbatical in Sweden where we worked at the University of Stockholm with Marianne Frankenhaeuser and her colleagues who were using hormone analysis to study occupational stress. On his return to Melbourne, Singer established the Brain-Behaviour Research Institute and, with Meredith Wallace at La Trobe University and Jack Bassett and me at Macquarie University, began a series of psychophysiological studies of occupational stress. Working together and independently we studied stress among factory and clerical workers, managers, shift-workers and aircraft cabin crew.

A study of female operators in a clothing factory found that workers subject to machine-controlled production processes had higher levels of adrenaline and noradrenaline than did workers on manually-operated machines which allowed more control over the work pace and greater utilisation of skills.[4] The results showed a hormonal increase for both manual and machine-controlled operators at the end of the working day. This is contrary to the normal twenty-four hour change pattern of the hormones in which levels should decline towards the end of the afternoon in preparation for rest and sleep during the evening. The hormonal patterns were reflected in the operators' questionnaire reports of an inability to unwind after work, which was the best predictor of job dissatisfaction and ill-health. The end of day arousal was much greater for the mechanised workers than for the manual workers, although this difference could only be detected by hormone analysis. None of the questionnaire responses revealed a difference which suggests that workers cannot explain to themselves or to others the origin of these feelings. In fact, a feature of this study was the high level of job satisfaction. The end-of-day hormonal levels in the clothing workers are probably a result of the fast pace originating in the incentive payment system (piece-rates). These results may constitute an early warning signal of the effects on health of mechanisation and payment-by-results systems.

The hormonal pattern of the clothing operators was then compared with that of women working in a munitions factory. Two similar levels of mechanisation were studied in both the clothing and munitions environments. While the clothing workers were paid by the piece, the munitions workers were paid a fixed wage. Results confirmed the prediction that the stress response, as measured by hormones in urine, would be greater under the piece-rate system than under the fixed-wage system. It is likely that working on a mechanised production system produces an increased stress response because of job overload. If so, stress is the result of mechanised work because, relative to manual work, operators would have difficulty in increasing the pace of production to take advantage of incentive payments. Workers would, therefore, have less control over production rates since they could modify only the input part of the production cycle. For this reason the higher stress levels were found among the workers who worked on the more highly mechanised systems on piece-rates.

In the middle-1980s jet aircraft were travelling long distances across time zones. Understandably, aircraft crews (and others) wondered about the stress effects of long-distance flying and jet-lag. High physiological cost of work is obvious in the case of jet-lag due to the two types of stressors associated with long-distance flights at high altitudes over different time zones. First, there are the physical stressors encountered during the flight (noise, cabin pressure, low levels of oxygen and humidity). Second, there is the problem of adjusting to circadian rhythms and sleep patterns resulting from different time zones.

At the request of the union representing aircraft cabin attendants, Jack Bassett and I studied the stressful effects of two QANTAS crews on a flight from Sydney to Los Angeles and return.[5] We reasoned that working on the flight was not likely to be associated with distress. While such factors as air turbulence, truculent passengers or general fatigue may influence feelings of well-being, it is more likely that distress, if experienced, would be due to jet-lag. Distress was assessed physiologically by urinary cortisol analysis and psychologically by mood ratings during a period which encompassed two days before, during and two days after the tour of duty. Two flights were studied with stopover times in Los Angeles of 56 and 84 hours in order to assess the different effects of adjustment to a new time zone.

The flight to Los Angeles did not involve an excessive physiological cost. While inadequate rest and dehydration were minor problems during the flight, they did not result in elevated levels of cortisol. But the period of time spent in Los Angeles was associated with increased levels of cortisol. It is possible that stressors associated with the incoming flight, such as fatigue and dehydration, may have contributed to the distress experienced during the stopover period. Such contribution, however, must have been small since after the return flight to Sydney all values rapidly returned to normal, even though the return flights appear to have been more stressful (based on cortisol levels) than the outward flights. The reason for the elevated cortisol levels and subjective reports of distress in Los Angeles is the disruption in circadian rhythm resulting from the change in night-day cycle. Individuals do not begin immediately to adjust to the alteration in day-night cycle and so there is a conflict between their biological clock and sensory information from the environment. The long-established circadian rhythms find themselves out of phase with the existing environment. Such an asynchronism in the cycles associated with major bodily function is extremely stressful and requires an adaptation time in the order of several cycle durations. This is the essence of jet-lag. Such a disruption in circadian rhythm, as experienced in Los Angeles, would be carried over into the return flight and would explain the greater distress experienced on that flight. Relationships between cortisol excretion and mood ratings also revealed the influence of jet-lag. The stopover period in Los Angeles and the flight home were characterised by fatigue and lack of vitality. As the effects of jet-lag accumulated, vitality and vigour decreased. The stressful effects of the tour of duty dissipated within two days.

A related problem for workers is shiftwork. George Singer and Meredith Wallace studied 900 electricity workers to establish the existence and nature of the difference between shift-workers and day-workers on factors relating to their quality of life.[6] Shift-workers reported more frequent occurrences of almost all health symptoms and experienced more 'nervous' problems. More shift-workers than day-workers reported receiving medical treatment for asthma, lung and breathing problems, stomach ulcers, arthritis and high blood pressure, but not for diabetes, cancer or heart disease. These health differences were not due to severe effects on a small proportion of shift-workers but rather moderate effects on a large proportion of the group studied. Shift-workers reported a more frequent use of laxatives, sleeping pills, pain-killers, cough medicines, tea, coffee, cigarettes and more dissatisfaction with their daily amount of sleep. In general, shift-workers perceived their health to be worse than others of the same age, worried more about their health and believed that work affects their health adversely. While shift-workers reported more interference to their family lives, especially in terms of the time available to spend with their families, they were not more likely to be divorced or separated from their spouses.

An unexpected finding was the response pattern of the shift-workers aged over 50 years. This group generally reported fewer problems than the other age groups and rarely differed significantly from the equivalent group of day-workers. This is in marked contrast to the 40–49 year age group where the largest differences between shift-workers and day-workers were found. The researchers interpreted the 50-year-old group as a survivor population, a group of workers relatively well adjusted to shiftwork.

The researchers also compared day-workers with previous and current shift-workers. The results showed that on health issues previous shift-workers were intermediate between day-workers and current shift-workers, suggesting the possible influence of lasting health deficits due to exposure to shiftwork. If shift-workers are a survivor population, then the previous shiftwork group includes those who have failed to survive and the effects of shiftwork may best be understood by an in-depth study of this group.

Meredith Wallace argued that the problem for shift-workers is that they attempt to work with inappropriate levels of hormones which may have a more immediate effect on health than prolonged exposure to stressful events. When adrenaline and noradrenaline levels are elevated the individuals are aroused and alert. If this peak occurs when shift-workers are trying to rest, they will probably experience sleep problems and related disorders. Enzymes involved in the digestive processes of the body also have rhythms and digestive and gastric problems can occur if these are out of phase. Adrenaline and noradrenaline levels suggested that afternoon shift-workers were irritable and tense when they began their shift. Night shift-workers showed a marked drop in adrenaline in the middle of the shift indicating a sluggish state not conducive to optimal performance, and their flat noradrenaline levels suggested that this hormone rhythm had not adjusted: the levels were as low as typically found during the sleep period of day-workers. Both night and afternoon shift-workers left work with adrenaline levels as high as day-workers, suggesting they may have been too alert for sleep shortly after work.

Wallace was interested in determining appropriate patterns of hormone levels for well-adjusted shift-workers. She argued that if workers maintain the pattern that is normal for afternoon and night their hormonal responses are tuned to rest when they need to be alert. If the job they are doing is the same as the day-workers, then the most appropriate pattern of hormonal response is the same as found in day-workers who have no health or work-related problems. This requires a complete twelve-hour shift in bodily rhythms.

George Singer argued that an essential first premise from local research is that greater affluence of shift-workers may be a necessary but not a sufficient condition for an improvement in quality of life.[7] More money may be essential for a higher material standard of living but it alone will not improve health and well-being. Shiftwork is a problem which must be solved by workers and managers through critical discussion. Changes will be of two types: redesign of jobs and re-design of shift-workers' life styles. Traditionally, managers oppose the first solution and trade unionists oppose the second.

Over the past forty years there has been considerable interest in the 12-hour, 3-day working week, particularly where it is an alternative to the 3×8 shift roster. The benefits include: fewer working days and longer blocks of time off work; savings in time and cost of travel to and from work; elimination of afternoon shifts; more time with family at important periods; better quality of sleep; improved quality of working life; less accumulated fatigue; no increase in administrative costs; long-term improvements in health. In an Australian study Wallace found that four months after the introduction of a 12-hour roster prolonged working time did not produce increased fatigue. Performance of power station operators on a simulated task showed that measures of speed and accuracy during 12-hour shifts were superior to those during 8-hour shifts. After two years there was no evidence of increased operator errors, work-related injuries or accidents. She also found that quality of sleep was significantly better for the 12-hour shift-workers and that most workers reported considerable satisfaction with the new rosters.[8]

The QANTAS and shiftwork studies used measures of stress hormones taken from urine which are difficult to collect during work. Jack Bassett, Pam Marshall and I decided, therefore, to use measures of cortisol taken from saliva. We designed a study to evaluate a number of physiological measures of stress with a sample of bank managers attending a residential training course. The stressor involved was the preparation and delivery of a fifteen-minute public lecture. Measurement of various hormones, heart rate and blood pressure were taken five times during the day of the lecture and on the following day. Rates of adrenaline were significantly elevated immediately following, but not before, the lecture. Salivary cortisol levels were significantly increased both immediately before and after the lecture while blood pressure and heart rate were unchanged. We concluded that salivary cortisol levels are the measurement of choice in human studies of stress where individual stressors can be identified.[9] We then turned our attention to the study of stress among senior managers.

While there have been innumerable questionnaire studies of stress among managers, psychophysiological studies are virtually unknown. Normally, senior managers experience relatively high levels of job demands and high levels of job control which suggests that distress levels in senior managers will be, on average, lower than for many other job categories. Nonetheless, managers are exposed to a range of organisational stressors which may accumulate through the working week which suggests that a linear relationship exists between passage through the week and levels of distress. However, other psychological factors, such as the Australian 'Monday syndrome' in which individuals claim to experience distress at the thought of a week's work ahead of them, suggest that the relationship between period in the week and distress is a negative one. A third possibility is that distress levels will peak in mid-week, reflecting cumulative distress unrelieved by the prospect of immediate rest and relaxation.

A study of senior managers at Telecom found that, relative to a rest-day baseline, cortisol excretion was significantly higher on Wednesday and on workday evenings.[10] Mood ratings showed that boredom and distress were associated with elevated cortisol levels and boredom was also associated with reported levels of illness. While we could not claim that certain managers were definitely at risk as far as stress-induced impairment of health is concerned, the elevated cortisol levels of the managers indicated an increased probability of stress-related disorders. The pattern of cortisol excretion through the working week offered no support to the advocates of the 'Monday syndrome'. Nor did our results support the cumulative distress model which predicted a linear relationship of increasing distress with increasing levels of cortisol throughout the week. We found that the relatively lower levels of cortisol on Friday afternoon suggested that the prospect of the weekend and the related diminution of work effort were associated with decreases in levels of distress. The relatively higher increases in cortisol on Wednesday pointed to a peak effort of work at mid-week some of which was experienced as distressing. Overall, we found that the changing patterns of cortisol through the week pointed to the situation-specific nature of the distress response. Obviously, the workplace provided obstacles and opportunities that were quite different from the home environment.

In an era of increased awareness of occupational stress and the difficulty of assessment related thereto, this study might be seen as a model for researchers, managers and employees who would like to see a more objectively rigorous approach to the topic. Sadly, because of the high levels of litigation associated with the RSI debacle, managers were disinclined to sponsor such research for fear that it would trigger another round of courtroom battles. To my knowledge, our psychophysiological study of senior managers was the first and last one of its type in Australia.

10

Rhetoric as Remedy

Counselling: The selling and buying of unwanted advice.

The conclusion from psychophysiological research into stress and distress is that the human body responds to environmental demands by activating specific hormones and other coping mechanisms. The human body is resilient and has the capacity to cope well with short-term demands. Chronic stress reactions, however, are danger signs and take two forms: unresolved practical problems in one's environment, or psychological problems about practical problems.

If stress is the body's reactions to environmental demands made on it to adapt and change, it is an inexorable aspect of human existence. The popularity of the movement built on stress, however, is not due to physiological studies or concepts. Rather, it is concerned with what is now called 'psychological injury'. If stressors are the practical problems of life, *psychological* problems – anxiety, hostility, depression – are second-order problems which are due to the way individuals perceive and respond to their practical problems. They are problems about problems. This was, as we have seen, the view of the ancient Stoics who based their philosophy on the idea that people are disturbed not by events but by the view they take of them.

Stoic philosophy appears in modern psychotherapy under the banner of Rational-Emotive Therapy (RET), also known as Rational-Emotive Behaviour Therapy. RET was invented by New York psychologist Albert Ellis who was ranked by the American Psychological Association (in 1982) ahead of Freud and behind Carl Rogers as the second most influential psychotherapist of the twentieth century. In a similar survey published in 2007 he was rated sixth.

Very few Australian managers had heard of Ellis until 1979 when Michael Bernard and I sponsored a lecture tour to Melbourne and Sydney respectively. His approach to the psychology of stress was so popular that his lectures were booked out; he was even featured on the front page of a Sydney newspaper because of the spectacle, witnessed by incredulous reporters, of several hundred managers standing and singing lyrics composed by Ellis and set to famous operatic arias. Since Ellis regarded neurosis as a fancy word for whining, he encouraged his audiences to sing: 'Life is unfair to me, whine, whine, whine; people treat me badly, whine, whine, whine.'

The experience of stress, according to Ellis, is followed by beliefs which, in turn, lead to emotional consequences. Distress is chiefly caused by self-defeating beliefs about oneself, others and the world's conditions. So when people are exposed to stressors they adopt either self-promoting or self-defeating beliefs. Beliefs are self-promoting if they help people solve or overcome their practical problems; beliefs are self-defeating if they inhibit effective problem-solving or prevent people from accepting those problems which cannot be solved. Ellis accepted that stress reactions are a natural and inevitable aspect of human existence. But he was not impressed by those who claim that such distressing emotions as anxiety, hostility, jealousy and depression are the inevitable consequences of environmental stressors. In short, we can be stressed but we do not have to become upset about it.

While the elimination of distress will not necessarily lead to happiness, it does lead to an enhanced ability to change conditions for the better, or to accept those conditions that cannot be changed. Motivation – moving toward a goal – is accompanied by rational, positive feelings (determination, enthusiasm) and rational, negative feelings (frustration, irritation). Negative feelings are rational and motivating because they provide one with the energy to move towards desirable goals and away from undesirable outcomes. But irrational feelings of distress sabotage one's ability to solve practical problems. It is rational to feel sad at the death of a friend; it is irrational to feel depressed. It is rational to feel irritated at a friend's unreasonable behaviour; it is irrational to feel hostile. And traumatic experiences are, in most cases, upsets and frustrations which people exaggerate and use strategically.

To understand RET it is useful to consider one of the specific techniques used to counteract an irrational belief. People become miserable for two reasons. First, they want to achieve a goal and feel disappointed and irritated when they do not achieve it. Second, they *demand* that they achieve this goal and feel bitter, enraged, anxious, despairing when they do not. It is important to note that there are healthy feelings of disappointment and irritation which are quite different from a childish refusal to accept a world with frustration and losses.

In the case of, say, a failed promotion a manager can respond rationally or irrationally. There is an Activating Event (A) (news of failed promotion). The manager tells himself 'It is unfortunate (or frustrating or disappointing) that I did not get this promotion.' This constitutes the Belief (B). Since the belief can be confirmed empirically it constitutes a Rational Belief (rB). The emotional consequence (rC) is one of regret or disappointment. Unhealthy, irrational feelings, however, result from the refusal to accept the world as a place where loss or disappointments occur. Thus, there is an Activating Event (A) followed by the manager telling himself that it is *awful* or *catastrophic* that he failed to gain a promotion. The terms 'awful' and 'catastrophic', when used in this context, mean more than unfortunate and since they have a surplus meaning which is not empirically supported they constitute an irrational belief (iB). This results in a radically different kind of emotional consequence ranging from mild to extreme upset (iC).

In his early books Ellis listed ten irrational, self-defeating beliefs which lead to poor performance:
- In order to be a happy person it is necessary to be approved of by almost everyone for virtually all that one does; and it is a catastrophic failure if one is criticised.
- In order to be worthwhile it is essential to be thoroughly competent in all possible respects.
- Certain people are basically wicked and should be severely blamed for their sins. One should be blamed (as opposed to being held responsible) for mistakes.
- In order to be happy one must never be frustrated and it is catastrophic when things do not go the way one would like them to.
- Happiness is externally determined and one has little ability to help rid oneself of negative feelings.
- If something is, or may be fearsome, one should be completely occupied with it.
- One needs someone stronger than oneself on whom to rely when making the decisions of life.
- One's past is all-important in determining one's happiness; because certain events once strongly affected one's life they must inevitably continue to do so.

– It is catastrophic if perfect solutions to the grim realities of life are not immediately found.

– Maximum happiness can be achieved by inertia, and by merely enjoying oneself.

In later books Ellis reduced to three the irrational ideas people use to upset themselves and others.

'I must be perfect and successful in everything I do or else I'm a worthless failure';

'People I care about must love and admire me and if they don't they deserve eternal damnation';

'The world must always treat me well and give me everything I want when I want it.'

In the 1970s Ellis teamed up with his friend Milton Blum to apply his psychotherapeutic theories and techniques to managers. In the book he subsequently wrote for managers he stated: '. . . although I am no great reader of books on the care and feeding of executives, I must say that the few I have read . . . have left me absolutely cold. For they generally tell you all the wise, winning and wonderful things an up-and-coming leader could and should do – *if* he were really capable of doing them. And they completely forget that he practically never is; and that, if he were, he probably wouldn't have much use for these books . . . Am I saying that the bright, often educated, up-and-coming young executive is just as crazy, and in some ways more so, than the average neurotic of modern times? I am.'[1] He argued that RET can help managers enhance decisiveness, increase efficient concentration, improve relations with others, achieve self-discipline, create self-acceptance, overcome feelings of hostility, conquer depression and attack and defeat all emotional upsets.

RET was widely embraced by Australian managers in the 1980s. Its robust, argumentative approach to problems in living appealed to those individuals who enjoyed confronting 'the tyranny of the shoulds'. It appealed more to males than to females who found the confrontational approach less to their liking than the client-centred approach associated with Carl Rogers. As the years rolled by, confrontational psychotherapies lost ground to client-centred therapies: clients were encouraged to express their feelings rather than argue. Rogers had his revenge on Ellis.

Originally developed by Rogers in the 1940s, client-centred therapy was based on the assumption that the potential of individuals is realised through relationships in which the counsellor communicates genuine acceptance, empathy and unconditional positive regard for clients. The assumption is based on Roger's view of human nature as one that strives towards self-actualisation. He believed that if individuals perceive in a therapeutic relationship genuine acceptance and empathy, the self-actualising capacity will overcome the restrictions which have been internalised in the process of living in a stressful world. To be true to themselves, counsellors must immerse themselves in the feelings of their clients and assess their own responses to those feelings. The task of the Rogerian counsellor is to facilitate clients' awareness and to trust in their own actualising processes. The attitudes of the counsellor create the optimal climate in which clients can allow their own growth to unfold.

Rogers believed that certain conditions must exist if personality change is to be effected. Two persons must be in psychological contact and one, the client, is vulnerable or anxious and the other, the counsellor, is responsive and expresses unconditional positive regard for the client. The counsellor experiences an empathic understanding of the client's internal frame of reference and endeavours to communicate this to the client thus achieving, to a minimal degree, unconditional positive regard.

Ellis had problems with these assumptions. That counsellors should literally feel their clients' disturbances or believe in their irrationalities is usually harmful rather than helpful to clients. Indeed, it is precisely the counsellor's ability to comprehend clients' immature behaviour without getting involved or believing in it that enables counsellors to induce clients to stop believing in or feeling that this behaviour is necessary. It is often the case that clients accuse the counsellor of being insufficiently attuned to their problems. Ellis's reply is to argue with them and show them how their attitudes and actions, including their anger, are illogical and self-defeating. After they have surrendered their irrational beliefs about the counsellor's lack of empathy, they frequently acknowledge that the counsellor might not have been as disengaged as they previously believed he was.

Managers who involve themselves in counselling face several dilemmas. First, they have to understand the metaphorical nature of everyday language. For example, some managers, with the support of psychologists, have claimed that their 'depression' was directly caused by their being passed over for promotion. A failed promotion is a *moral* dilemma not a quasi-medical condition. However, a conspicuous feature of postmodern life has been the progressive medicalisation of moral conflicts in which metaphorical illnesses are treated as literal illnesses. When people describe themselves as 'sick', 'burned out' or 'nervy', counsellors are embroiled in a linguistic game and they have to decide whether their client is speaking literally or metaphorically. In the case of psychological problems such descriptions are metaphors – people who speak like this are not literally sick, burned out or nervy.

Counsellors are expected to be able to distinguish between literal and metaphorical pronouncements. Since this is no easy matter when it comes to people who prefer to describe themselves metaphorically, it is not surprising that many prefer the literal interpretation. Just as women who expressed unacceptable ideas were once thought to be possessed by evil spirits and burnt alive at the stake, so today people who behave eccentrically are frequently thought to be suffering from a personality disorder. Dancing in a cemetery is eccentric. Digging up dead bodies is eccentric, but it is also illegal. If people act eccentrically we can laugh at them, ignore them, chastise them, and so forth. If people act illegally they face the legal consequences of their actions. Not satisfied with these two categories, psychiatrists added a third – personality disorder or 'flawed personality'. In this case the label is applied to individuals whose (legal) behaviour annoys, upsets or offends others. The notion of a personality disorder has the added advantage of relieving individuals of responsibility for their actions on the grounds that the 'flaw' in their personality, rather than their choices, caused them to act as they did.

Counsellors who value personal autonomy do not accept the idea of a flawed personality. Nor do they accept the idea that personality traits are internal forces which cause people to behave as they do. They quickly realise, however, that many people do not wish to surrender this comforting idea and resist a therapeutic language based on personal choice and responsibility. And so counsellors find themselves caught up in a language game based on the idea of heteronomy and related notions of oppression and depression, patienthood and victimhood. The crucial point in the therapeutic encounter occurs when counsellors and clients argue about such fundamental interpretations of human behaviour because the counsellor's commitment to autonomy or heteronomy determines its future course. Obviously counsellors can use arguments for ignoble ends, to obfuscate and confuse clients. They may even argue merely to demonstrate their rhetorical skills. Counsellors who promote autonomy, however, use argument to free clients from coercion and inhibition, oppression and depression, not to confuse and restrict them.

There are clearly other functions of language which may facilitate or inhibit personal development. After all, one does not live by argument alone. A familiar example is the wedding ceremony where, at a crucial point in the proceedings, bride and groom are asked to commit themselves in the language of willing – 'I will'. One likes to think that at this important moment in the ceremony bride and groom will not argue with each other, or simply share their feelings. Two people pass from a state of engagement – a promise to marry – to the state of marriage by public declaration. They could argue about details, although it is generally assumed that this process has taken place before the wedding, and will certainly occur after it.

The modern obsession with personality disorders is indicative of the degree to which we live in a postmodern world which is regulated by passionate denials of personal freedom and responsibility. We are, as Austrian satirist Karl Kraus noted, profoundly enmeshed in grammatical confusions and we cannot be freed without first being extricated from the extraordinary variety of metaphors which hold us captive. This is especially true of the language of personality disorder which is so elastic as to accommodate almost any meaning one attaches to it. Personality disorder can refer to an emotional upset occasioned by failing to get what one wants, or a feeling of despondency dignified by the word 'depression'.

The number of 'official' personality disorders, as enumerated in the *Diagnostic and Statistical Manual of Mental Disorders – IV-TR,* has increased dramatically in the past fifty years. These include: anti-social, avoidant, dependent, histrionic, narcissistic, obsessive-compulsive and paranoid personality disorders.

Australian managers are in the firing-line of competing and contradictory claims about the status of personality disorders. It is clear that the term has various meanings and that psychologists have been unable to define the term adequately. I suggest that the notion of personality disorder has outlived whatever usefulness it may have had and should be dispensed with in the fields of counselling and management.

It remains a stubborn fact that managers are increasingly called upon to deal with psychological as well as practical problems at work. While the notions of personality and personality disorders are unhelpful, managers need to know something of the language and practice of counselling if they are to address psychological issues, formally or informally. Whether they like it or not, Australian managers have been forced into the role of 'physician of the soul'.

The idea that 'physicians of the soul' are concerned with rhetoric rather than medicine, conversation rather than cures, was familiar to the ancient Greeks. In ancient epic poetry suggestive, cheering speeches are used for curative purposes. The persuasive word was considered so important in ancient Greece that it was applied 'technically' to the solving of problems in living. Psychological counselling, then, began as 'therapeutic oratory' based on rhetoric. It was clear to Plato that rhetoric – persuasive speech – was the treatment used by physicians of the soul while physicians of the body healed by dietary and biological means. In the *Phaedrus* Plato has Socrates say that medicine imparts health and strength by the giving of medicine and food while rhetoric implants the conviction of virtue by the right application of words. In Plato rhetoric is therapeutic when it produces an internal harmony which is achieved by strengthening the will and reorganising beliefs, a process known as *Katharsis*.

The idea that to have power over language is to have control of oneself and others is deeply embedded in human thought. We see this in the way great orators are criticised as base rhetoricians or praised as noble ones. The base rhetorician uses language to deprive individuals of their liberty, responsibility and dignity; the noble rhetorician uses language to encourage individuals to speak clearly, think for themselves, question and make the choices that commitment to responsible living requires. The characterisation of rhetoric as noble or base depends on whether rhetoricians are judged to influence others toward what is good or bad, a judgement that will differ according to the values of those who render it.

Counsellors are rhetoricians, whether they appreciate it or not. When counsellor and client interact they attempt to influence each other to see or to do things. The persuasive element in the relationship is what qualifies the actions of one or both parties as fundamentally rhetorical. For example, the way in which counsellors offer advice to clients is an exercise in rhetoric.

In the play *Voyage Round my Father*, the author John Mortimer has a father say: 'I never give advice, it's far too precious.' He proceeds to describe alternative courses of action for his son to consider. Mortimer is sensitive to the difference between telling people what they *should* do and offering behavioural alternatives for their evaluation. To give advice is to adopt a particular ethical position and to recommend it to others and while counsellors' ethics may be widely shared in their milieu, they can never be assumed to apply to all individuals therein.

The giving of advice by those in positions of power is not a benign affair, particularly when those to whom the advice is directed are often distressed or distressing, coerced or coercing. French moralist La Rochefoucauld wrote: 'Nothing is less sincere than the way people ask and give advice. The asker appears to have differential respect for his (counsellor's) sentiments, although his sole object is to get his own approved and transfer responsibility for his conduct; whereas the giver repays with tireless and disinterested energy the confidence that has been placed in him, although most often the advice he gives is calculated to further his own interests or reputation alone.'[2]

While most people like freedom because it increases their choices, they dislike responsibility because it commits them to some action against which they may be judged. The ancient Greeks saw responsibility as a 'response to the rights of others' which was based on a promise to honour obligations toward certain individuals. The Greek notion of responsibility is not based on commandments: it was a personal, moral response to freedom, an idea that has been modified by the rise of powerful religious and scientific authorities.

The language of responsibility, expressed through promises, merges with the language of personal power and has the potential to liberate individuals from their compulsions, anxieties and resentments: it develops and extends autonomy. Base rhetoric, on the other hand, transforms the language of responsibility into the language of resentment and bad conscience. Many people reject autonomy as a means to security and a base from which they coerce themselves (bad conscience) or others (resentment). Counsellors know only too well that such people do not respond positively to arguments which challenge their view about personal helplessness. Learned helplessness is a powerful strategy and difficult to modify by argument. Consequently, counsellors often prefer to avoid difficult rhetorical exchanges in favour of the rhetoric of the expert. But this compromises a basic goal of autonomous counselling: clients should learn to evaluate for themselves by challenging external commands and advice about how and what to evaluate. The autonomous counsellor, therefore, refuses to tell clients that they should change. Promising is the responsibility of clients; honouring promises their mark of distinction.

Counsellors who value and promote autonomy encourage promising, argument and cooperation. They assume that responsibility and freedom are inseparable and encourage their clients to discover that the obligations implied by a response to autonomy are more congenial and productive than those implied by a coerced response to dubious authority.

In her analysis of counselling styles, Elizabeth Collins found that the majority of Australian managers in her study tried to avoid involving themselves with the psychological problems of their colleagues.[3] When they did act as counsellors their style was generally non-confrontational and empathic rather than confrontational and argumentative. It was primarily a 'safe' relationship in which they could not be accused of invalidating colleagues' problems. The general view among managers was that they should 'lend a sympathetic ear' and provide encouragement and support. While her survey results showed that some managers did indeed use argument and confrontation, usually when employees did not change or respond positively to their interventions, none was prepared to acknowledge this during her interviews. Their preferred style was closer to Rogers than to Ellis.

The counselling style of Australian managers reflects a humanistic approach to management which emphasises the importance of the social needs of employees and the importance of soft-skills in dealing with them. Collins found that while managers stated at interview that the responsibility for solving personal problems rests with employees, many were prepared to engage in counselling and used a style which was non-directive, supportive and pragmatic. All managers acknowledged the primacy of organisational requirements and so the risk taken by managers who challenge employees was judged to be less than the risk involved in failing to fulfil organisational expectations. In other words, it is more serious to challenge an organisation than an employee. A few managers who expressed a preference for traditional management practices took the position that work is not an appropriate place to discuss personal, psychological issues and thereby refused to involve themselves in psychological counselling. They were probably wise to do so.

Epilogue

No academic field has been more popular since 1950 than has psychology, and although there is often progressive disenchantment, considerable numbers of graduates have been produced. During the whole of this time the discipline has been dominated by the US where psychologists have pretended to be scientists. The most remarkable feature of this is that the assumptions of 'scientific psychology' are the same as the basic tenets of Puritanism: absence of freewill, absolute determinism and the derogation of subjective experience. Underlying this is the belief that human behaviour operates on scientific laws and must therefore yield to scientific analysis.

It cannot be shown, a priori, that this model will give an exhaustive account of the nature of human beings; but it can equally be claimed that it cannot be shown that it will not do so. 'Scientific' psychologists, including personologists, can therefore insist that interpretation of events within the model is the only officially acceptable form of explanation, even when rival explanations are possible. Masses of behavioural data are therefore collected and interpreted in mechanistic terms. This mass of interpretation gradually creates the impression that the assumptions must be true if a system developed upon them can 'explain' so much. And at this point it is clear that psychology becomes propaganda – propaganda for a model of human beings living in a society of rationalised action devoted to a philosophy of power.

No one who listens to personologists can have any doubt that their aim is to understand and control human behaviour. Human beings are to be 'constructed' so as to fit the bureaucratic order of society. Psychology of this type is to be the agent of the economic bureaucracy in creating a modern synthesis between itself and the psychological structure of its recruits.

Underlying the behaviour of psychomanagers, and the psychologists' aim of helping them control the behaviour of subordinates, is the unexpressed faith that an increase of managerial power is sufficient to solve organisational problems. The history of management is alone sufficient to cast doubt on the wisdom of placing much faith in this assumption. Power concentrated in managerial groups becomes relatively unresponsive to human values since there is no internal dynamic which guarantees that its use shall be benign. The powers of individuals, on the other hand, are to an unprecedented degree under the direction of managers rather than under the direction of an ethic based on the value of human beings as such, and the first care of managers is so to direct their colleagues as to protect and enlarge their own power. People today find themselves in the position of those who cannot avoid participating in the generation of formidable amounts of managerial power, but are unable to devise adequate means for its control. They are therefore unable to secure themselves against the possibility of its being used against them. This is especially the case when psychologists become servants of power and use their skills to manipulate and control people.

Recently, a distinguished professor of psychology, Kevin R Murphy, compiled a list of industrial psychology's greatest 'hits and misses'.[1] His list is based on the opinions of his colleagues and his personal experience of the field. His list of successes includes: the growth of the field, the scientist-practitioner model, measurement and statistical analysis and meta-analysis of cognitive tests. His 'misses' or failures, if true, represent a serious indictment on the profession.

1. Industrial and organisational psychologists, he noted, continue to act as servants of power and focus on management and large organisations.

2. Meta-analyses of the validity of personality tests as predictors of job performance have shown that 'the sort of broad personality traits that were the focus of meta-analytic research in the 1990s and beyond generally show quite low levels of predictive ability, and they look good only in comparison with previous assumptions that showed no validity whatsoever.'

3. While emotional intelligence consultants are doing a booming business, 'most of the attention-grabbing claims regarding EI are either exaggerated or completely wrong. There is little credible evidence that emotional intelligence is an important or unique predictor of performance, or that it is more important than cognitive ability in predicting *any* broad criteria. While there are some potentially interesting ideas in the EI literature, the concept has not lived up to the hype.'

4. 360-Degree feedback is another 'hot' topic in management. Its naïve advocates promote the view that multiple parties should be involved in providing feedback on performance. Murphy points out the obvious fact that performance ratings from different sources almost always contradict each other. 'These (360-degree) systems seem to be built for failure. They will typically produce discrepant feedback and will provide users with solid reasons to ignore much of the negative feedback they receive.'

5. Maslow's hierarchy of needs remains one of the most popular theories in the management psychological literature. Yet, Murphy acknowledges that none of its key ideas has received empirical support, nor is it likely that such support will be forthcoming in future research. Weaknesses of the Maslow model have been well known for over forty years, but the model remains popular. 'Like creationism and intelligent design theories, Maslow's model seems to be sustained mainly on the basis of people's assumptions about what *should* be true, not by the evidence. It is well past time to drop this relic from I/O psychology textbooks.'

6. Another popular topic – organisational climate – is based on a metaphor. Do organisations have climates, or do people talk as if they do? Can we actually take the temperature of an organisation as some writers have suggested? 'Organisational climate' is like 'emotional intelligence': both terms are metaphorical, conceptually inadequate and empirically unsupported. After years of fruitless research, their days are, or should be, over.

Australian managers have for many years danced with psychologists who claim that they can 'get inside' individuals in order better to understand their personalities. The ancient philosophers were not so naïve. They knew that one can only understand oneself and others in terms of the *relationships* in which we are inexorably involved. There is no such thing as personality, if by that term we mean some internal source of power which makes us what we are. As Shakespeare said, we are actors in the drama of life and we can only be understood as role-players who are influenced by the rules and rewards of our community. When psychologists and psychomanagers ignore or dismiss roles, rules and rewards in an attempt to uncover personality, we have before us emperors with no clothes – or indeed no emperors at all.

References

Chapter 1: A Weird Country

1   D H Lawrence, *The Letters of D H Lawrence*, Vol 4, (eds. W Roberts, J Boulton & E Mansfield), Cambridge: Cambridge University Press, 1987, pp263–264.

2   T Collins (1903), *Such is Life*, Hawthorn: Lloyd O'Neil, 1970, p371.

3   H Heseltine, 'The Australian Image: The Literary Heritage', in C Semmler (ed.), *Twentieth Century Australian Literary Criticism*, Melbourne: Oxford University Press, 1967, p101.

4   N Lindsay, *Creative Effort: An Essay in Affirmation*, London: Cecil Palmer, 1924, pp4–7.

5   N Lindsay, 'Australia and Australians', in K Wingrove (ed.), *Norman Lindsay: On Art, Life and Literature*, St. Lucia: University of Queensland Press, 1990, pp83–90.

6   J Docker, *Australian Cultural Elites: Intellectual Traditions in Sydney and Melbourne*, Sydney: Angus and Robertson, 1974, ppix–x.

7   H Lawson, *Collected Verse*, Vol 1, (ed. C Roderick), Sydney: Angus & Robertson, 1967, p261.

8   R Ward, *The Australian Legend*, Melbourne: Oxford University Press, 1958, pp1–2.

9   B O'Reilly, *Green Mountains* (1940), South Yarra: Lloyd O'Neil, 1983, pp96–97.

10 Quoted in D Jones & B Andrews, 'Australian Humour', in L Hergenhan (ed.), *New Literary History of Australia*, Ringwood: Penguin, 1988, pp61, 67, 68.

11   P O'Farrell, *The Irish in Australia*, Sydney: UNSW Press, 1993, pp18–21.

12   J Ross, *The Myth of the Digger: The Australian Soldier in Two World Wars*, Sydney: Hale & Ironmonger, 1985, p175.

13   W K Hancock, *Australia*, London: Ernest Benn, 1930, p183.

14   A-M Moodie, *Local Heroes: A Celebration of Success and Leadership in Australia*, Sydney: Prentice-Hall, 1998, quotes pp18, 103–104, 139, 146, 157.

15   L Murray, *The Quality of Sprawl: Thoughts about Australia*, Sydney: Duffy & Snellgrove, 1999, pp1–2.

Chapter 2: Managers And Mates

1   D Horne, *The Lucky Country*, Harmondsworth: Penguin, 1971, pp71–73.

2   H Stretton, 'The Quality of Leading Australians', *Daedalus*, 1985, 114, pp197–230.

3   J Marshall & R Trahair, *Industrial Psychology in Australia to 1950: An Annotated Bibliography*, Bundoora: La Trobe University Library, 1981.

4   S Encel, *Equality and Authority: A Study of Class, Status and Power in Australia*, Melbourne: Cheshire Publishing, 1970, pp412–415.

5   G Hofstede, *Culture's Consequences: International Differences in Work-Related Values*, London: Sage Publications, 1980.

6   G W England, *The Manager and His Values: An International Perspective*, Cambridge, MA: Ballinger, 1975.

7   G Renwick, *A Fair Go for All: Australian/American Interactions* (eds. R Smart & D Henderson), Yarmouth ME: Intercultural Press, 1991.

8   R Spillane, 'Attitudes of Business Executives and Union Leaders to Industrial Relations', *Journal of Industrial Relations*, 1980, 22, 3, pp317–326.

9   C Hampden-Turner & F Trompenaars, *Building Cross-Cultural Competencies*, Chichester: John Wiley, 2000.

10   G Henderson, 'Not Much Enterprise in Karpin Report', *Sydney Morning Herald*, 16 May, 1995, p13.

11   F Emery, 'Karpin Taskforce Manages to Get Confused', *Business Review Weekly*, 24 July, 1995, p72.

12   D Stove, *The Plato Cult and Other Philosophical Follies*, London: Basil Blackwell, 1991, p31.

13   J Martin & J Ray, 'Anti-Authoritarianism: An Indicator of Pathology', *Australian Journal of Psychology*, 1972, 24, 1, pp13–18.

14   D Stove, ibid., p168.

15   I Palmer & C Hardy, *Thinking about Management: Implications of Organizational Debates for Practice*, London: Sage Publications, 2000, Ch.10.

16   P F Drucker, *Management: Tasks, Responsibilities, Practices*, New York: Harper & Row, 1974, p370.

Chapter 3: Drucker and Friends

1   P F Drucker, *Adventures of a Bystander*, London: Heinemann, 1979, pp256–293.

2   P F Drucker, 'The Coming Rediscovery of Scientific Management', in *Towards the Next Economics and other Essays*, London: Heinemann, 1981, pp96–106.

3   A Carey, 'The Hawthorne Studies: A Radical Criticism', *American Sociological Review*, 1967, 32, p416.

4   K Lewin, R Lippitt & K White, 'Patterns of Aggressive Behaviour in Experimentally Created "Social Climates"', *Journal of Sociology*, 1939, 10, pp271–299.

5   A Carey, 'Industrial Psychology and Sociology in Australia', in P Boreham, A Pemberton & P Wilson (eds.), *The Professions in Australia: A Critical Appraisal*, St. Lucia: University of Queensland Press, 1976, p238.

6   For details and references see R D Lansbury & R Spillane, *Organisational Behaviour: The Australian Context*, (2nd ed.), Melbourne: Longman Cheshire, 1991, pp101–105.

7   P F Drucker, 'Have Employee Relations Policies had the Desired Effects?' *American Management Association, Personnel Series*, 1950, 134, p7.

8   P F Drucker, 'The Unfashionable Kierkegaard', in *The New Markets and other Essays*, London: Heinemann, 1971, pp44–58.

Chapter 4: Motivation and Manipulation

1   J W Hunt, *Managing People at Work: A Manager's Guide to Behaviour in Organizations*, London: McGraw-Hill, 1979, pp5–6.

2   S Andreski, *Social Sciences as Sorcery*, Harmondsworth: Penguin, 1974, p69.

3   R D Lansbury & R Spillane, *Organisational Behaviour: The Australian Context*, Melbourne: Longman Cheshire, 1991, pp255–279.

4   D Clutterbuck & G Bickerstaffe, 'Where Have all the Management Gurus Gone?' *International Management*, January 1982, pp12–15.

5   P F Drucker, 'Behind Japan's Success', *Towards the Next Economics and Other Essays*, London: Heinemann, 1981, pp164–180.

Chapter 5: The Personality Cult

1   B F Skinner, *About Behaviorism*, Harmondsworth: Penguin, 1993, p178.

2   H De Cieri & R Kramar, *Human Resource Management in Australia*, Sydney: McGraw-Hill, 2008, p290.

3   W H Whyte, *The Organization Man*, Harmondsworth: Pelican, 1969, pp373–378.

4   A M Paul, *The Cult of Personality: How Personality Tests are Leading Us to Miseducate our Children, Mismanage our Companies, and Misunderstand Ourselves*, New York: Free Press, 2004, p128.

5   M R Barrick & M K Mount, 'The Big Five Personality Dimensions and Job Performance: A Meta-Analysis,' *Personnel Psychology*, 1991, 44, pp1–26.

6   For details of this case I have drawn heavily on E Alderman & C Kennedy, *The Right to Privacy*, New York: Alfred A Knopf, 1995, pp277–290.

Chapter 6: Unintelligent Intelligence

1   L Spillane, 'Language and Values: Communication Styles of Australian Public Service Managers', *Australian Journal of Public Administration*, 1994, 53, 1, pp63–66.

2   R Nozick, *Philosophical Explanations*, Oxford: Clarendon Press, 1981, pp4–13.

3   B Russell, *History of Western Philosophy*, London: George Allen & Unwin, 1946, p491.

4   M Viroli, *Machiavelli*, Oxford: Oxford University Press, 1998, pp9–10.

Chapter 7: The Leadership Myth

1   W J Byrt, *Leaders and Leadership*, Melbourne: Sun Books, 1978, pp5–6.

2   M Weber, *The Theory of Social and Economic Organisation*, Oxford: Oxford University Press, 1947.

Chapter 8: The RSI Debacle

1   Workers Compensation Commission of NSW, *Compensation Reports New South Wales,* Vol XLVII, Government Printer NSW, 1973, piv.

2   J Mathews & N Calabrese, 'Guidelines for the Prevention of Repetitive Strain Injury (RSI)', *Health and Safety Bulletin*, 1982, 18, pp1–33.

3   R Spillane & L Deves, 'RSI: Pain, Pretence and Patienthood', *Journal of Industrial Relations*, 1987, 29, pp41–48.

4   M Quinlan & P Bohle, *Managing Occupational Health and Safety in Australia*, Melbourne: Macmillan, 1991, p126.

5   R Spillane & L Deves, 'Psychological Correlates of RSI Reporting', *Journal of Occupational Health & Safety – Australia & New Zealand*, 1988, 4, pp21–27.

6   B Hocking, 'Epidemiological Aspects of "Repetition Strain Injury" in Telecom Australia', *Medical Journal of Australia*, 1987, 147, pp218–222.

7   Y Lucire, *Constructing RSI: Belief and Desire*, Sydney: UNSW Press, 2003.

Chapter 9: Occupational Stress

1   S C Ouelette-Kobasa, 'Inquiries into Hardiness', in L Goldberger & S Bregnitz (eds.), *Handbook of Stress: Theoretical and Clinical Aspects*, New York: Free Press, 1993, pp77–100.

2   R Karasek, 'Job Socialisation and Job Strain: The Implications of Two Related Psychological Mechanisms for Job Design', in B Gardell & G Johansson (eds.), *Working Life: A Social Science Contribution to Work Reform*, Chichester: Wiley, 1981, pp75–94.

3   J R Bassett, 'Psychological Stress and the Coronary Artery in Ischaemic Heart Disease', in S Kalsner (ed.), *The Coronary Artery*, London: Croom Helm, 1982, pp474–500.

4   N Romas et al., 'Measuring Physiological Stress Responses: The Effects of Factors in the Work Environment on Urinary Catecholamine Responses', *Journal of Occupational Health & Safety – Australia & New Zealand*, 1987, 3, 5, pp515–523.

5   J R Bassett & R Spillane, 'Jet Lag as an Occupational Stressor', *Journal of Occupational Health & Safety – Australia & New Zealand*, 1985, 1, pp26–32.

6   M Wallace (ed.), *Shiftwork in Australia*, Bundoora, La Trobe University: Brain-Behaviour Research Institute, 1985, pp10–21.

7   G Singer, 'Future Options in the Shiftwork Arena', In M Wallace, ibid., pp22–23.

8   M Wallace (ed.), *Managing Shiftwork*, Bundoora, La Trobe University: Brain-Behaviour Research Institute, 1989, pp49–76.

9   J R Bassett, P Marshall & R Spillane, 'The Physiological Measurement of Acute Stress (Public Speaking) in Bank Employees', *International Journal of Psychophysiology*, 1987, 5, pp265–273.

10   J Bassett, B Hocking & R Spillane, 'Cortisol Excretion and Illness Reporting: A Psychophysiological Study of Business Executives at Home and at Work', *Journal of Occupational Health & Safety – Australia & New Zealand*, 1998, 14, 2, pp135–141.

Chapter 10: Rhetoric as Remedy

1   A Ellis, *Executive Leadership: A Rational Approach*, Secaucus, NJ: The Citadel Press, 1972, pp10–13.

2   La Rochefoucauld (1665), *Maxims*, (trans. L Tancock), Harmondsworth: Penguin, 1959, p52.

3   E A Collins, *Counselling Styles of Australian Managers*, Unpublished MA Thesis, Sydney: Macquarie University, 1997.

Epilogue

1   K R Murphy, 'Organisational Psychology's Greatest Hits and Misses: A Personal View', in A I Glendon, B M Thompson & B Myors, *Advances in Organisational Psychology*, Bowen Hills, Qld: Australian Academic Press, 2007.

Index